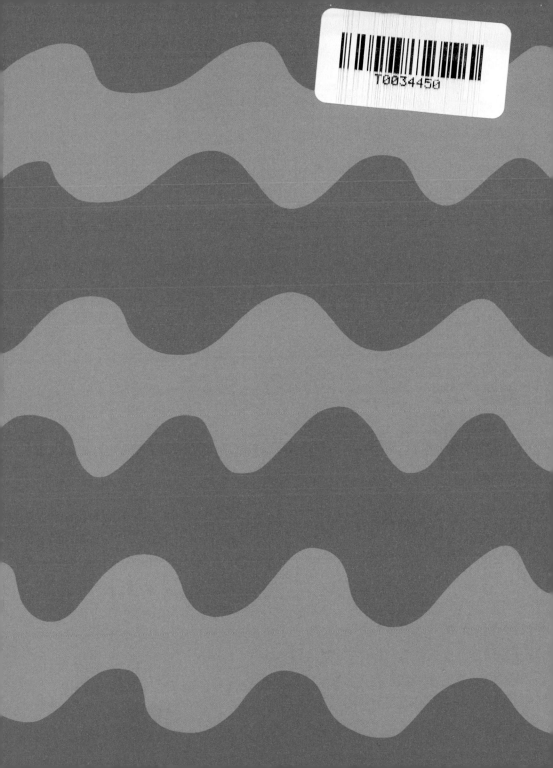

Sip Me, Baby, One More Time

Cocktails Inspired by Pop Music's Iconic Women

ASHLEY GIBSON

Running Press
PHILADELPHIA

Text copyright © 2024 by Ashley Gibson
Interior and cover photographs copyright © 2024 by Alyson Brown
Cover copyright © 2024 by Hachette Book Group, Inc.

Running Press
Hachette Book Group
1290 Avenue of the Americas, New York, NY 10104
www.runningpress.com
@Running_Press

First Edition: April 2024

Published by Running Press, an imprint of Hachette Book Group, Inc. The Running Press name and logo are trademarks of Hachette Book Group, Inc.

The Hachette Speakers Bureau provides a wide range of authors for speaking events. To find out more, go to www.hachettespeakersbureau.com or email HachetteSpeakers@hbgusa.com.

Running Press books may be purchased in bulk for business, educational, or promotional use. For more information, please contact your local bookseller or the Hachette Book Group Special Markets Department at Special.Markets@hbgusa.com.

The publisher is not responsible for websites (or their content) that are not owned by the publisher.

Print book cover and interior design by Justine Kelley.
Illustrations by Justine Kelley.

Library of Congress Cataloging-in-Publication Data
Names: Gibson, Ashley (Writer on cocktails), author.
Title: Sip me, baby, one more time : cocktails inspired by pop music's most iconic women / Ashley Gibson.
Description: First edition. | Philadelphia : Running Press, [2024]
Identifiers: LCCN 2023018819 (print) | LCCN 2023018820 (ebook) | ISBN 9780762483624 (hardcover) | ISBN 9780762483631 (ebook)
Subjects: LCSH: Cocktails. | LCGFT: Cookbooks.
Classification: LCC TX951 .G437 2024 (print) | LCC TX951 (ebook) | DDC 641.87/4—dc23/eng/20230424
LC record available at https://lccn.loc.gov/2023018819
LC ebook record available at https://lccn.loc.gov/2023018820

ISBNs: 978-0-7624-8362-4 (hardcover), 978-0-7624-8363-1 (ebook)

Printed in China

APS

10 9 8 7 6 5 4 3 2 1

CONTENTS

INTRODUCTION

In 2019, I lost my corporate nine-to-five job and became a stay-at-home mom for a year before returning to work. And, naturally, while I was out of work, I had an identity crisis. A lot of my sense of self-worth had come from my job, and without it, I felt lost. But something that always brought me back and made me feel like myself again was a delicious meal paired with a beautiful cocktail. When the pandemic began in 2020, my best friends and I could no longer meet up at a bar, so I started making my own cocktails at home and FaceTiming them instead, while we blasted our favorite pop songs and danced together from a distance.

Fast-forward to when things started opening back up: We realized that not only were we saving money by making drinks and dancing in our homes, but we were having more fun, too. We didn't have to fight off skeevy guys interrupting us—we could truly just connect with each other over drinks and the queens of the music industry. I kept making drinks at home, and eventually I started filming the process so that others could do it, too. I was having the time of my life creating drinks for my close-knit group of friends, and through that hobby I found an online community of like-minded people who also appreciate the mood boost of a gorgeous cocktail paired with a well-crafted pop song. I decided to write this book to spread that love even further.

Welcome to *Sip Me, Baby, One More Time*, where your dreams of photo shoot–worthy drinks are 100 percent achievable in the comfort of your own kitchen. These recipes can be made by anyone, from the broke college student who wants to host a pregame party with her best friends before a night out to the exhausted mother who deserves a relaxing and beautiful beverage after a three-hour bedtime battle. And if alcohol isn't your jam, you can omit the booze and have a gorgeous mocktail that feels like just as much of a treat.

As a former broke college student and now a mother myself, I have been on a decade-long quest to find the most beautiful cocktails, only to realize I can make them myself using ingredients found in most grocery or liquor stores. I can make the classics, like a great old-fashioned or a negroni, but I can also craft an original, simple, elegant, gorgeous, and/or garnished work of art—and you can, too.

With a great drink in your hand and the perfect song playing, you can transform any place into your own personal party. In my experience, pop music is unmatched when it comes to capturing a feeling and conjuring a vibe we can all relate to. That's why this book is inspired by the greatest songs from the women who define this genre, as well as some lesser-known up-and-coming artists whose music is as exciting to me as stumbling upon a new favorite liqueur that adds just the flavor I've been missing.

Sip Me, Baby, One More Time combines the art of cocktail making with the power of these artists to create an experience curated by emotion. Each chapter of this book is dedicated to a specific feeling—from coping with soul-crushing heartbreak to feeling as if you want to hop on a table and dance it out—and is filled with easy-to-make, beautiful cocktails dedicated to songs from top female artists.

So get out the edible glitter, put on your cutest dress OR your comfiest pajamas, fire up your portable speaker, and call up your best friends. It's time to make some amazing drinks.

A NOTE ON SERVING SIZES:

Each drink recipe serves one, unless otherwise specified. To make more than one, you can just multiply the quantity of each ingredient by the number of drinks you'd like to make.

SPECiAL MATERiALS & INGREDiENTS

I've designed these drinks to look *and* taste great, so the recipes include a few special touches.

ICE MOLDS

Ice molds are inexpensive, and cute ice cubes add so much pizzazz to a drink. You can look for fun ice molds at online retailers like Amazon, home-goods stores such as Williams-Sonoma or Bed Bath & Beyond, and sometimes even your local dollar store.

GARNISHES

Garnishes can elevate a regular ol' cocktail into an absolute work of art. My favorite garnishes are:

- Fresh flowers (make sure they're food-safe and free from harmful chemicals)
- Food-grade dried flowers (available online or at some grocery stores)
- Dried citrus (available online or at some grocery stores, or you can make your own at home by thinly slicing citrus and placing in a 200°F oven for about 3 hours)
- Luxardo maraschino cherries, the ONLY maraschino cherries worth buying, in my opinion (available online or at grocery stores)
- Butterfly pea tea for a pop of color (available online or at some grocery stores)

BITTERS

Someone once described bitters to me as the "seasoning" of a cocktail. Bitters are optional, but they add a lot of interesting flavor. I buy most of mine from El Guapo Bitters, a women-owned business and online store that operates out of Louisiana. I used to think bitters were only for harsh, stereotypically "masculine" drinks until I discovered El Guapo.

GLASSWARE

It is my personal belief that countless beautiful cocktails can be made with a set of only seven cocktail glasses: a coupe glass, a beer can glass, a martini glass, a rocks glass, a shot glass, a highball glass, and a wineglass. Glassware is surprisingly inexpensive, and I've purchased mine from Amazon, CB2, Dollar Tree, and local antique and thrift shops. If a drink calls for a glass different than one of the seven listed here, one of these can easily do the trick.

EDIBLE GLITTER

This one speaks for itself. There is nothing that elevates the appearance of a cocktail more than edible glitter, and it's so satisfying to watch it swirl around in your drink. I purchase glitter from the brand Fancy Sprinkles, and you can also find it on Amazon or in specialty baking shops.

AQUAFABA VERSUS EGG WHITES

Some of these recipes call for egg whites (use pasteurized eggs to avoid the risk of salmonella), but if you don't consume eggs, aquafaba can be used in their place. Aquafaba is the liquid from a can of chickpeas and can be strained from the can and used in cocktails for the same effect. Egg whites and aquafaba both create a foamy texture at the top of the cocktail and are essentially tasteless. (And if the thought of including either one of these grosses you out, you can always skip it entirely!)

SYRUPS

Syrups are my favorite part of making cocktails and instantly elevate their flavors. I feel like a little potions master, running around my kitchen throwing fruits, herbs, spices, and even candies into boiling pots of water and sugar. The thought of making my own simple syrup used to terrify me. But one day I needed some and my only option was to make it myself, and I was stunned by how straightforward it was. Thus, my love of syrup making began.

Cocktail syrups can also be store-bought, but nothing compares to homemade, and making your own is so easy and fun. All you have to do to make syrup is combine 1 cup of sugar, 1 cup of hot water, and however much of whatever flavor you want. For example, strawberry syrup would be: 1 cup sugar, 1 cup water, 5 mashed strawberries (based on my own preference, but you do you!).

To make these syrups, pour the sugar and water into a pot and let it come to a boil. Add your flavoring and let the mixture simmer for 10–15 minutes. Then strain it into a jar, let it cool completely, and put it in a sealed container in the fridge for later. It's really that simple—no pun intended!

SIMPLE SYRUP

1 cup water

1 cup sugar

Blackberry Syrup

1 cup water

1 cup sugar

4–5 blackberries

Blueberry Syrup

1 cup water

1 cup sugar

7–8 blueberries

Bubblegum Syrup

1 cup water

1 cup sugar

10 pieces of bubblegum

Note: The color of the syrup depends on the bubblegum you use. If your syrup isn't turning pink, you can add a splash of grenadine for color.

Cinnamon Syrup

1 cup water

1 cup sugar

3–4 cinnamon sticks

Gummy Worm Syrup

1 cup water

½ cup sugar

4–5 purple/blue gummy worms

Hibiscus Syrup

1 cup water

1 cup sugar

½ cup dried hibiscus flowers (easily found on Amazon)

Hot Honey Syrup

1 cup water

¾ cup honey

3–4 slices of your preferred hot pepper (jalapeño, habanero, etc.)

Jalapeño Syrup

1 cup water

1 cup sugar

4–5 jalapeño slices (depending on how much spice you want)

Jalapeño Dragonfruit Syrup

1 cup water

1 cup sugar

½ cup frozen dragonfruit, mashed

4–5 jalapeño slices (depending on how much spice you want)

Lavender Syrup

1 cup water

1 cup sugar

1½ ounces food-grade lavender

Marigold Syrup

1 cup water

1 cup sugar

5–6 food-grade marigold flowers

Marshmallow Syrup

1 cup water

¼ cup sugar

4–5 marshmallows

Mint Syrup

1 cup water

1 cup sugar

4–5 mint leaves

Peach Syrup

1 cup water

1 cup sugar

3 fresh peaches (pitted)

Persimmon Syrup

1 cup water

1 cup sugar

1 peeled and chopped persimmon

Raspberry Syrup

1 cup water

1 cup sugar

7–8 raspberries

Rose Syrup

1 cup water

1 cup sugar

¼ cup food-grade dried rose petals

Spiced Cinnamon Syrup

1 cup water

1 cup sugar

2 whole cloves

1 whole star anise

2 cinnamon sticks

Star Anise Syrup

1 cup water

1 cup sugar

2–3 whole star anise

Sweet Potato Syrup

1 cup water

1 cup sugar

¼ cup canned sweet potato puree

Vanilla Syrup

1 cup water

1 cup sugar

1 tablespoon vanilla extract

HEART BREAK

Heartbreak is an inevitable part of life. No matter what kind of loss you are grieving, this playlist has got you covered. Whether someone broke your heart, you broke someone else's heart, or you're breaking your own heart, there's a song and a cocktail or two on this playlist just for you.

One of the best things about pop songs is the way they awaken feelings that all of us can relate to, even if we haven't had the exact experiences the songs describe. These songs can apply to breaking up, losing a friend, going through parental issues, grieving what could have been, or grieving the loss of a job or even an identity.

Healing comes with time and community. Embrace the pain and blast this playlist with your best friends while sipping these cocktails, eating ice cream, scarfing down a charcuterie board, or wallowing in your sadness.

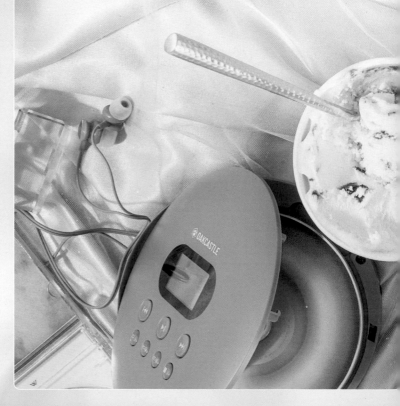

PLAYLIST

All Too Well (10 Minute
Version) (Taylor's
Version) (From the
Vault), Taylor Swift
3
SAD GIRL SANGRIA

Everytime,
Britney Spears
5
FEELING BLUE VODKA SHOT

Skin and Bones,
070 Shake
6
DEATH IN THE AFTERNOON
COCKTAIL

Easy On Me,
Adele
7
RED WINE SPRITZER

favorite crime,
Olivia Rodrigo
9
GIN GUMMY WORM SOUR

Flowers, MARINA
11
MARIGOLD GIN COCKTAIL

Liability, Lorde
12
DARK 'N' STORMY

ghostin,
Ariana Grande
13
WHITE CHOCOLATE
VODKA COCKTAIL

Nobody Gets Me,
SZA
14
OCEAN TEARS RUM AND
COCONUT

Ready to Go,
Noah Cyrus
15
SWEET POTATO HOT TODDY

Maroon, Taylor Swift
17
CARNATIONS TO ROSES
BLACKBERRY GIN MARTINI

Norman fucking
Rockwell, Lana Del Rey
19
FRENCH 75

doomsday,
Lizzy McAlpine
20
NECROMANCER COCKTAIL

Heartbreaker,
Mariah Carey
23
EUPHORIC AND WEAK
LEMON-LIME GIN COCKTAIL

All Too Well (10 Minute Version) (Taylor's Version) (From the Vault)

Taylor Swift

SAD GIRL SANGRIA

When Taylor Swift's album *RED* came out in 2012, "All Too Well" was a standout track for every Swiftie (including me). It was a lyrical remedy for anyone who was heartbroken, vulnerable, and ready to process devastating loneliness and rejection. Taylor made us feel *seen* in our suffering with her brilliantly specific descriptions of universal emotions; she let us know we weren't alone. When the fandom caught wind that there was an unreleased ten-minute version of this song, we refused to shut up about it, and after almost ten years of begging, Taylor released the extended track and somehow made an already iconic song even more iconic.

I'll never forget how I stayed up way too late the night the song came out, listening to it over and over again, dissecting each lyric. It took me back to the heartbreak and loneliness that I felt when listening to the original in 2012, and her new verses also brought forth new feelings for me in 2021. There was more anger, truth, and transparency, the perspective of a more empowered woman in her thirties who was taking control of her entire narrative. I hope any young person who's been hurt by someone can one day feel the raw power of unleashing those emotions.

So when you're feeling lost, play this song on repeat and make this sad girl sangria. This is the ultimate autumn drink: the cider, apples, cinnamon, and cloves add a touch of coziness that you can wrap yourself in like a favorite scarf. You can even warm this drink on the stove to take the comfort to the next level. This recipe makes 4–5 glasses.

---

1 bottle (750 ml) pinot noir

1½ cups apple cider

2 Honeycrisp apples (thinly sliced)

4 whole cloves

2 cinnamon sticks

Red edible glitter (optional)

Pour pinot noir and apple cider into a pitcher. Add Honeycrisp apples, cloves, cinnamon sticks, and glitter, then stir. Refrigerate for at least 30 minutes before serving.

If heating: Place all ingredients in a large pot and simmer for 30 minutes.

Everytime
Britney Spears
FEELING BLUE VODKA SHOT

Britney might be best known for her upbeat dance tracks, but this mournful classic is my favorite Britney song. It came out when I was only fourteen, but I've carried it with me into adulthood, and I still play it whenever I feel heartbroken. Although Britney is singing to someone she lost as a romantic partner, the heart-wrenching openness of "Everytime" speaks to me when I'm experiencing any kind of loss.

Sometimes when you're heartbroken, you just need a shot of vodka to perk you up. This shot is easy to make even when you're feeling blue, and the color is the exact hue I see in my head when I hear this song.

---

1 ounce vodka

¼ ounce blue curaçao

¼ ounce lime juice

Blue edible glitter

Place vodka, blue curaçao, lime juice, and blue edible glitter in a cocktail shaker. Shake for 20 seconds, then strain into a shot glass.

Skin and Bones
070 Shake
DEATH IN THE AFTERNOON COCKTAIL

Why not distract yourself from your own heartbreak with a song *about* heartbreak that somehow makes you forget you're heartbroken for 3 minutes and 33 seconds? This song is as ethereal as an absinthe buzz, and, when paired with the first sip of this cocktail, it will numb you just enough to illuminate your mind. For greater effect, make a couple of these cocktails and put the song on repeat.

1 ounce absinthe

½ ounce Simple Syrup (page XIII)

4 ounces Champagne

Pour absinthe and simple syrup into a coupe glass. Top with Champagne.

Easy On Me

Adele

RED WINE SPRITZER

This song speaks to anyone who has tried and tried so hard and become so exhausted that they've finally given themselves permission to give up. It's for those moments when the hard truth can't be ignored anymore.

It also speaks to the part of yourself that gets lost when you devote everything you have to other people instead of your own happiness. This song was released when I was going through a similar situation, and I went on a drive just so I could blast it in my car and sob.

This drink takes little effort, so it's perfect if you, too, have given up, at least for the moment. Adele's voice sounds the way red wine tastes, so this spritzer fits perfectly with her heartbreaking ballad. The freshness of the oranges and mint adds an earthy element to this drink in honor of our Taurus Earth goddess, Adele.

---

1 (6-ounce) can club soda

Pinot noir

Orange slices

Mint sprigs (for garnish)

In a wineglass, pour club soda, then top with the desired amount of pinot noir. Add orange slices, then garnish with mint sprigs.

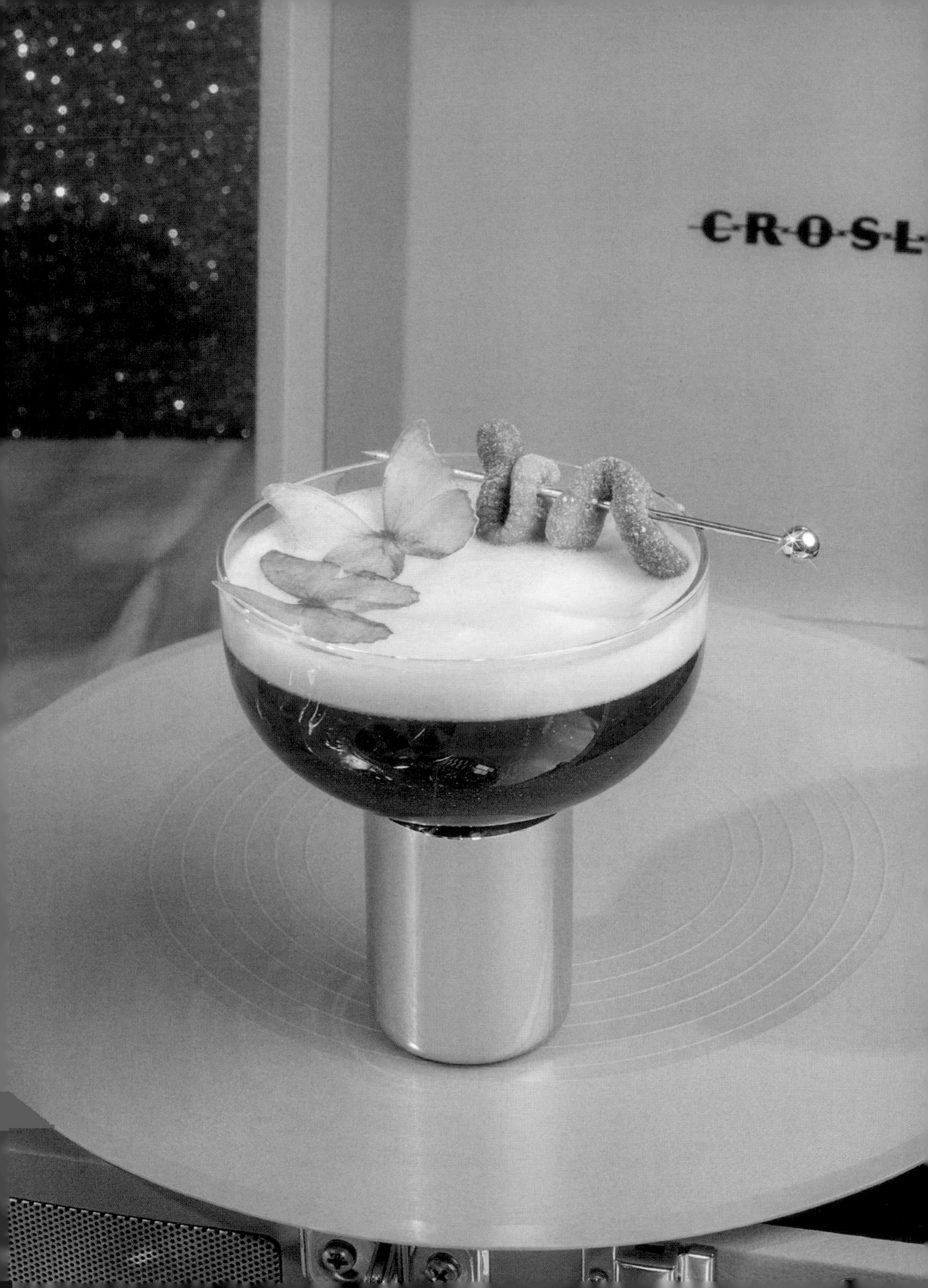
CROSL

favorite crime
Olivia Rodrigo
GIN GUMMY WORM SOUR

This song beautifully describes how we can be coerced into betraying ourselves (and sometimes other people) for someone we think we love. We trick ourselves into thinking all is fair, but we know it isn't. We scream into our pillows, yearning to receive in return a fraction of the effort we've shown for the other person. When the feelings are still fresh and raw, we look back and hope that we were the person's "favorite crime." But in our hearts, we can't help but acknowledge how much the person used us.

This fun, bright drink contrasts with the sadness of this song. Just like the love Olivia is describing, it's bittersweet. Sometimes a beautiful, colorful drink is just the thing to distract us from the darkness swirling in our hearts. This one is also a tribute to the youthful, effervescent aesthetic of Olivia Rodrigo's iconic debut album *SOUR*, which featured this song. Who can be sad when there are gummy worms around?

1½ ounces Empress gin

1 ounce freshly squeezed lemon juice

1 pasteurized egg white or ½ ounce aquafaba

Purple edible glitter

¼ ounce Gummy Worm Syrup (page XIV)

Edible butterfly wafers (for garnish)

Gummy worms (for garnish)

In a cocktail shaker, place gin, lemon juice, egg white or aquafaba, purple edible glitter, and gummy worm syrup. Dry-shake for 30 seconds, then shake with ice for 30 seconds and strain into a coupe glass.

Garnish with edible butterfly wafers and gummy worms.

Flowers

MARINA

MARIGOLD GIN COCKTAIL

Sometimes, in relationships, one person gets careless and stops putting in effort; that chips away at what once was. If your lover had just done one simple thing differently, then maybe the relationship could have been salvaged.

When someone has failed to give you flowers, aka failed to do that one simple thing in the relationship that you needed, make your own flower (syrup) and enjoy this cocktail.

---

2 ounces botanical gin

1 ounce freshly squeezed lemon juice

1 ounce Marigold Syrup (page XIV)

Marigold flowers (for garnish)

In a cocktail shaker, place gin, lemon juice, and marigold syrup. Shake with ice for 30 seconds. Strain over ice into a collins glass. Garnish with marigold flowers.

Liability

Lorde

DARK 'N' STORMY

If you've ever felt like you were too much for someone (who hasn't?), this song and cocktail pairing is for you. Why is it such a universal experience to have felt this way? Like you're just a "liability"? Sometimes, you're made to feel like a fun and exciting commodity until things start to get real, and then you're treated like a storm that the other person needs to run from.

When you're afraid that you're too wild and untamed, treat yourself to this hearty, warming cocktail and remember that just like a dark 'n' stormy, you're a classic. The people who deserve you will think you're just enough.

---

2 ounces dark rum

4 ounces ginger beer

¼ ounce Cinnamon Syrup (page XIV)

Dried lime wheel or fresh lime wedge (for garnish)

Place rum, ginger beer, and cinnamon syrup in a rocks glass and stir to combine. Garnish with a dried lime wheel or a fresh lime wedge.

ghostin

Ariana Grande

WHITE CHOCOLATE VODKA COCKTAIL

Grief is arguably the form of heartbreak that can bring the most torment. And breaking someone else's heart can hurt just as much as having your own heart broken. This song encapsulates both of these all-consuming feelings. It's about being with someone who you know isn't right while you grieve the loss of someone else, and trying to convince both the person you're with now and yourself that everything will be okay, even when you don't know that.

White roses often represent grieving the loss of a loved one. The color of this drink mimics a white rose. The white chocolate liqueur and crème de cacao offer a hint of sweetness, because sweetness can be found in almost every tragedy we endure.

Corn syrup (for rimming the glass)

Pink sanding sugar (for rimming the glass)

1½ ounces white chocolate liqueur

1½ ounces white crème de cacao

½ ounce vodka

2½ ounces half-and-half

White rose (for garnish)

Sugar rim:

Roll the rim of a martini glass in corn syrup, then dip it into pink sanding sugar.

Cocktail:

Combine white chocolate liqueur, crème de cacao, vodka, and half-and-half in a cocktail shaker. Shake well, then strain into the martini glass. Garnish with a white rose.

Nobody Gets Me
SZA
OCEAN TEARS RUM AND COCONUT

I am always in awe of artists' ability to share their deepest feelings through their art. Feelings I wouldn't dare expose to the world, they broadcast with such bravery. This song is a perfect example. We have all felt the kind of awful, shameful wanting it describes, but SZA was bold enough to put it in the form of a song for everyone to hear. We all have that one person who gets us as no one else does, and daring to imagine them with anyone but us is so painful that it's almost unbearable. I'd take a physical ailment any day over a broken heart.

For this drink, I was inspired by SZA's *SOS* album cover. SZA sits out over the ocean—heartbroken, I assume, since this album is full of heartbreak. The dark blue glitter turns this cocktail into an ocean of tears for you to gulp down when you feel like nobody but that *one* person gets you.

---

1 ounce blue curaçao

2 ounces pineapple juice

2 ounces coconut water

1 ounce white rum

Dark blue edible glitter

Pour blue curaçao, pineapple juice, coconut water, white rum, and edible glitter into a rocks glass over ice and stir well.

Ready to Go

Noah Cyrus

SWEET POTATO HOT TODDY

Transitioning into the acceptance stage of heartbreak can be the most difficult part, especially if you're stubborn, like me. This song has us reflect on accepting when we know someone wants to go and then actually letting them. There is strength in knowing when to give up and not chasing after someone who already has one foot out the door.

Knowing when to let something go doesn't just apply to romantic relationships. That deep feeling of knowing can apply to a job, a friendship, a familial relationship. We know when we are dragging something out for far too long; we often deny it until we can't anymore and then we finally let them go and we are free.

Noah's folksy sound makes me want to sip Tennessee whiskey with honey. This drink goes down easy, just like Noah's smooth voice. The honey and sweet potato syrup add a sweetness that feels as sweet as it does when we finally let go. The heat of this drink warms a cold, broken heart.

---

6 ounces water

1½ ounces whiskey

¼ ounce honey

1½ ounces Sweet Potato Syrup (page XV)

1 cinnamon stick (for garnish)

In a teakettle or saucepan, bring water to a boil, then pour into a mug. Add whiskey, honey, and sweet potato syrup and stir well. Garnish with a cinnamon stick.

Maroon

Taylor Swift

CARNATIONS TO ROSES BLACKBERRY GIN MARTINI

In this song, Taylor anchors the memories of a tumultuous lost love through a brilliant fixation on shades of red—most significantly, maroon. Remembering those passionate feelings through the precise shade they invoke really makes you feel like you're there in the scene.

The beginning of this song feels like the beginning of a relationship when everything is euphoric. As the song continues, we can feel the relationship growing darker, just like the color maroon. I'm reminded of lost love, and I wonder if the other person can still taste it in the cabernet.

In this moody cocktail, the tart flavor of the blackberry syrup hits you like the passion of a new connection. And as you sip the drink, the rose melts, symbolizing the slow end of one.

---

1 bag hibiscus tea (for ice cubes)

1½ ounces gin

1 ounce freshly squeezed lime juice

1 ounce Aperol

1 ounce Blackberry Syrup (page XIV)

Maroon edible glitter

Rose-shaped ice:
Brew hibiscus tea. Let the tea cool, then pour into a rose ice mold. Freeze overnight.

Cocktail:
Place rose-shaped ice into a coupe glass. Combine gin, lime juice, Aperol, blackberry syrup, and edible glitter in a cocktail shaker with ice. Shake well, then strain over the rose ice into the glass.

Norman fucking Rockwell

Lana Del Rey

FRENCH 75

This song feels like one big eye roll at male fragility. Lana unapologetically eviscerates the muse of this song in such a calm manner that it almost feels sad, but what I really think she feels is indifference.

When you've arrived at the indifferent stage of your journey, you know it's over. You see the person for who they truly are: a "goddamn man child" who makes bad art and blames all their misfortunes on other people.

Lana evokes old Hollywood, so when I listen to her music, I like to sip on a classic. This take on a French 75 cocktail, with its refreshing hint of lemon and ritzy Champagne, pairs perfectly with Lana's classic voice.

---

2 ounces London dry gin

½ ounce lemon juice

1 teaspoon superfine sugar

5 ounces chilled brut Champagne or dry sparkling wine

Lemon rind twist

Put ice, gin, lemon juice, and sugar in a shaker. Shake well. Strain over ice in a collins glass (or no ice into a Champagne flute), top off with Champagne, and garnish with a lemon rind twist.

doomsday

Lizzy McAlpine

NECROMANCER COCKTAIL

This song's brilliant use of metaphor eloquently describes a relationship with a narcissist. Lizzy softly begs her tormenter to pull the plug on the relationship, but she also asks the person to wait a little longer and to make it painless so that she can retain some semblance of control. But it seems as if she has given up all of her agency; she feels so powerless that she's just waiting for this person who has controlled the entire relationship to control the ending as well. She builds to the peak of the song, when she sings about her ultimate death: There are no friends or family present, only her "murderer."

This song is for anyone who has been controlled, finessed, and isolated into a slow, torturous, symbolic death. When that death comes, it's devastating, but it's also incredibly freeing. Even when you're buried so deep, you can still breathe more easily than when you were suffering in the relationship.

This classic necromancer cocktail is perfect for waking you from the dead.

¾ ounce absinthe

¾ ounce elderflower liqueur

¾ ounce Lillet Blanc

Dash dry gin

¾ ounce lemon juice

Lemon rind twist (for garnish)

Place absinthe, elderflower liqueur, Lillet Blanc, gin, and lemon juice in a cocktail shaker with ice and shake well. Strain into a coupe glass. Garnish with a lemon rind twist.

Heartbreaker

Mariah Carey

EUPHORIC AND WEAK LEMON-LIME GIN COCKTAIL

I wanted to finish out this chapter on a lighter note because there is always joy to be found, even in heartbreak. With "Heartbreaker," Mariah turns heartbreak into the most fun bop of the century. *Rainbow* is one of my all-time favorite albums; I played it repeatedly during my middle school years. I *know* I drove my mom crazy blasting this album at the highest volume my little stereo could manage. Whether I was happy or heartbroken from puppy love, I had this album on repeat and memorized every lyric.

This drink is bright, fun, and the perfect antidote to a broken heart. Why not turn your heartbreak into a colorful, campy, glittery potion and have a little laugh at yourself for running back "incessantly" to your heartbreaker?

Red sanding sugar

Orange sanding sugar

Yellow sanding sugar

Green sanding sugar

Blue sanding sugar

Corn syrup

1½ ounces Empress gin

½ ounce elderflower liqueur

½ ounce lemon juice

2 ounces Sprite

Red heart-shaped lollipop (for garnish)

Sugar rim:

Sprinkle red, orange, yellow, green, and blue sanding sugar onto a plate in a circle. Rim a highball glass with corn syrup, then roll the glass into the sanding sugar to create a rainbow. Set aside.

Cocktail:

Mix gin, elderflower liqueur, and lemon juice in a cocktail shaker and shake well. Strain into the highball glass over ice. Top with Sprite. Garnish with a red heart-shaped lollipop.

CHAPTER
2

FURY

There is so much power in anger, and this playlist encapsulates the force of female rage. Whether you're dealing with difficult coworkers, annoying family members, or a man who had the actual *audacity*, this playlist and drinks lineup will not only get you through it but help you come out guns blazing. Every melody is full of feminine fury. Ready to enter your villain era? Put this playlist on and drink up.

Most of the recipes in this chapter are shots—because what feels more powerful than downing a shot without flinching?

PLAYLIST

Happier Than Ever,
Billie Eilish
27
HOT HONEY COCKTAIL

I am not a woman,
I'm a god, Halsey
29
CINNAMON WHISKEY SHOT

Mother's Daughter,
Miley Cyrus
30
LEMON HONEY
WHISKEY SHOT

Power & Control,
MARINA
31
PURPLE LEMON GIN SHOT

I Did Something Bad
(Taylor's Version),
Taylor Swift
33
BLACK GLITTER
OLD-FASHIONED

Pink Venom,
BLACKPINK
35
DRAGONFRUIT MARGARITA

Bitch Better Have My
Money, Rihanna
37
KAMIKAZE SHOT

Womanizer,
Britney Spears
38
GIN ELDERFLOWER
PROSECCO COCKTAIL

Cocoon, 070 Shake
39
PAINKILLER COCKTAIL

Kill Bill, SZA
41
PINEAPPLE MARTINI

breadwinner,
Kacey Musgraves
43
WHISKEY AMARETTO
CRANBERRY SHOT

Piece of Me,
Britney Spears
44
HOT PINEAPPLE SHOT

Fighter,
Christina Aguilera
45
JALAPEÑO POMEGRANATE
MIX

Son of a Gun (I Betcha
Think This Song Is
About You),
Janet Jackson
47
DRY MARTINI

That Don't Impress Me
Much, Shania Twain
49
PINEAPPLE-RUM FRUIT
PUNCH COCKTAIL

Happier Than Ever

Billie Eilish

HOT HONEY COCKTAIL

We all want to believe that people are good. Ignorance truly is bliss, and denial sometimes wins out. But please know that no one with a heart would ever make you relate to this song.

The kind of person Billie confronts in this cathartic song is the type who will mess with your mind for years until you've invested so much of yourself into feeding your own denial that you don't know what to do with your pent-up rage.

Let Billie be your inspiration. Mix up this bracing, fiery cocktail and reclaim your power.

½ ounce Hot Honey Syrup (page XIV)

2 ounces gin

¾ ounce freshly squeezed lemon juice

Chili pepper (for garnish)

Pour hot honey syrup, gin, and lemon juice into a cocktail shaker. Shake for 30 seconds. Strain into a coupe glass and garnish with a chili pepper.

I am not a woman, I'm a god

Halsey

CINNAMON WHISKEY SHOT

Halsey herself said this is not a woman power anthem. To me, it's an anthem for the power that comes from confronting who you really are, even the parts you're not proud of. The more you sit with discomfort, the less you fear it. With that insight comes accepting that every person's character exists on a spectrum, and that no one is fully good or bad. That realization, like listening to "I am not a woman, I'm a god," empowers me and humbles me all at once.

This shot is simple and straightforward, but it doesn't go down easy, just like this song. And it hits hard—again, just like this song. The more you take in of each, the more intense they get.

1½ ounces whiskey

½ ounce cinnamon schnapps

Combine whiskey and cinnamon schnapps in a cocktail shaker over ice. Strain into a shot glass.

Mother's Daughter

Miley Cyrus

LEMON HONEY WHISKEY SHOT

In my opinion, this is Miley's best and most underrated song. I felt so empowered when I heard it for the first time, and I still do every time it comes on. Like Miley, I derive my strength and power from the women in my family—my mom, my aunt, my grandma, and all the other women who came before me.

I also love how Miley reclaims negative stereotypes that women have tried to fight for centuries: nasty, evil witches. You think I'm a nasty, evil witch? Then back up because I'll show you just how nasty I can be.

Take this sweet, no-nonsense shot, reclaim the negative words thrown at you, and know you've got the power.

½ ounce freshly squeezed lemon juice

½ ounce honey

1 ounce whiskey

Lemon wedge (for garnish)

Combine lemon juice, honey, and whiskey in a cocktail shaker. Shake well and strain into a shot glass. Garnish with a lemon wedge.

Power & Control
MARINA
PURPLE LEMON GIN SHOT

The silver lining of experiencing true fury is stepping into your feminine power. Once you've reached your breaking point and hit your limit for being treated like shit, you begin to realize that you have *all* the power because you get to choose what you're willing to tolerate. No one is above you, and it's so much easier to leave people who think they are in the dust where they belong when you've come to this realization. Your vulnerability, femininity, and softness are strengths, too.

This simple but magical shot turns from blue to purple as you squeeze in the lemon juice. This shot is easy to make for your coven of furious women who are fed up with the emotional labor.

---

2 ounces freshly squeezed lemon juice

1 ounce Empress gin

1 ounce Simple Syrup (page XIII)

Combine lemon juice, gin, and simple syrup in a cocktail shaker with ice. Strain into a shot glass.

I Did Something Bad (Taylor's Version)

Taylor Swift

BLACK GLITTER OLD-FASHIONED

I love this song so much because Taylor plays such a relatable character. We all have an alter ego, the alternative self who is unafraid of exacting revenge, exposing others, and being the villain—and even celebrating it. Sometimes, doing something bad *does* feel so good, and it's empowering to realize how much power we hold within ourselves. If we wanted to burn it all to the ground, we could.

This drink screams the aesthetic of the *Reputation* album; it's a twist on an old-fashioned (Taylor's favorite drink), and the dark, glittery look exemplifies having fun while being a little twisted.

---

1 sugar cube

½ orange slice

2 maraschino cherries

¼ teaspoon agave

2 dashes bitters

3–4 drops black gel food coloring

Black edible glitter

Ice cube made with a square ice mold

1½ ounces whiskey

Club soda

Square ice cube:
Freeze water in a square ice mold overnight.

Cocktail:
Muddle a sugar cube, an orange slice, maraschino cherries, and agave in a rocks glass. Add bitters, a few drops of black gel food coloring, and black edible glitter, then muddle again. Add a square ice cube and whiskey, and top with club soda.

Pink Venom

BLACKPINK

DRAGONFRUIT MARGARITA

The spooky taunting at the beginning of this song really sets the tone for the female villain archetype the BLACKPINK girls embody in their performance. Anthems for women villains are my absolute favorite genre; nothing gets me more fired up than a woman singing about getting her own. In this song, the women of BLACKPINK enact their evil plan of enchanting others with their pink venom.

Jalapeño dragonfruit syrup is a bright, gorgeous pink color, the exact color I imagine pink venom to be. Of course, the jalapeño is there to add the spice that this song delivers.

---

1 ounce freshly squeezed lime juice, plus more for rimming the glass

Hawaiian-style black salt (for rimming the glass)

1½ ounces tequila

1½ ounces Jalapeño Dragonfruit Syrup (page XIV)

Lime sparkling water

Lime slice (for garnish)

Salt rim:
Rim a wineglass with lime juice. Pour Hawaiian-style black salt into a bowl and dip the glass into the salt to coat the rim. Set aside.

Cocktail:
Combine tequila, 1 ounce of lime juice, and the jalapeño dragonfruit syrup in a cocktail shaker. Shake well and strain into the prepared wineglass. Top with lime sparkling water. Garnish with a lime slice.

Bitch Better Have My Money

Rihanna

KAMIKAZE SHOT

Nothing makes me feel like I'm hot shit quite the way this song does. I turn into an absolutely feral criminal when it comes on. If there's any way I want to feel when I'm furious, it's powerful. Sometimes, it's hard to stick up for ourselves and get what we're owed, but Rihanna makes it just a little bit easier with this song.

Rihanna sings, "Kamikaze, if you think that you gon' knock me off the top," so what better to pair with this anthem than a kamikaze shot? Fantasize about getting revenge while blasting this song and taking this shot.

1½ ounces vodka

½ ounce triple sec

Green edible glitter

½ ounce freshly squeezed lime juice

Lime wedge (for garnish)

Combine vodka, triple sec, green edible glitter, and lime juice in a cocktail shaker with ice. Shake well and strain into a shot glass. Garnish with a lime wedge.

Womanizer
Britney Spears
GIN ELDERFLOWER PROSECCO COCKTAIL

Circus was the album that defined my college years, the most formative period of my life. The whole album is a huge ego boost, which is something young women coming into their femininity and bursting into adulthood need, and thank *God* for Britney for giving it to us.

Britney calls out "players" in this song, the men (and women!) who think they can tell everyone the same sweet nothings and get away with it forever. The ones who use the same manipulative tactics on every vulnerable person who crosses their path. Britney isn't fooled, and this song is a warning to us that we shouldn't be fooled, either. But even the wisest of us will fall for a trick every now and then, and this song is the perfect antidote, the rage anthem we can blast when we've figured out who someone truly is.

I wanted to evoke the gold in the *Circus* album cover with the lovely essence of this drink. And you can never go wrong with prosecco, in my opinion! Prosecco makes me feel like I'm on top of the world, even if I'm drinking a cheap bottle. With this drink fizzing in my hand and "Womanizer" blasting in my headphones, I'm a furious and fancy queen.

---

1 ounce gin

1½ ounces elderflower liqueur

¾ ounce freshly squeezed lemon juice

3 ounces prosecco

Lemon peel (for garnish)

Combine gin, elderflower liqueur, and lemon juice in a cocktail shaker and shake well. Strain into a Champagne glass. Top with prosecco and garnish with a lemon peel.

Cocoon

070 Shake

PAINKILLER COCKTAIL

This song is about telling your truth, setting yourself free, and leaving someone who is unable or unwilling to grow with you to rot in their own mediocrity. Accepting that someone isn't who you thought they were can be a grueling process, but once you finally free yourself from that person's venomous grasp, it's like breaking out of a cocoon. Now you're the butterfly and you can fly away, leaving them behind in their own echo chamber of averageness.

070 Shake sings about taking painkillers as part of the healing process in this song, so, naturally, I have to pair it with my go-to version of a painkiller cocktail.

---

2 ounces rum

4 ounces pineapple juice

1 ounce freshly squeezed orange juice

1 ounce cream of coconut

Place rum, pineapple juice, orange juice, and cream of coconut in a cocktail shaker. Shake well, then strain into a hurricane glass.

Kill Bill

SZA

PINEAPPLE MARTINI

If some man with the actual audacity has never made you feel close to homicidal, consider yourself blessed. As someone whose sadness quickly turns to anger, I relate to this song a little too much. I am so thankful that SZA wrote this song so we can fantasize about going homicidal to soothe our pain, rather than committing heinous crimes IRL. My favorite part is when she ups the insanity and sings that she did it all for love. She's her most unhinged self in this song and I LOVE IT.

This drink was heavily inspired by the "Kill Bill" music video, which was in turn heavily inspired by the movie *Kill Bill*. The yellow pays homage to Uma Thurman's yellow suit in the movie, and the red is all for SZA.

Red gel food coloring (for decorating the glass)

2 ounces vodka

1½ ounces pineapple juice

1½ ounces coconut cream

¼ ounce Jalapeño Syrup (page XIV)

½ ounce lime juice

Pineapple wedge (for garnish)

Sliced jalapeños or sweet peppers (for garnish)

Decorate the glass:

Decorate a martini glass with red gel food coloring. Make it look like blood— get creative! I like to make a line just below the inside of the rim and let it drip a little bit. You can decorate the glass before you pour the drink, or do it after if you don't want a lot of food gel getting into the drink. The more gel that gets in the drink, the more red-orange color it will have; it's up to you.

Cocktail:

Combine vodka, pineapple juice, coconut cream, jalapeño syrup, and lime juice in a cocktail shaker and shake well. Strain into the decorated martini glass. Garnish with a pineapple wedge and the pepper of your choosing. If a jalapeño is too spicy, a sweet pepper works beautifully.

breadwinner

Kacey Musgraves

WHISKEY AMARETTO CRANBERRY SHOT

Being a breadwinner doesn't necessarily mean earning the most money in the household in the literal sense. In this raw anthem, Kacey sings about being the breadwinner in a relationship by being the one who has the "shimmer," the one who makes the other partner feel better about themselves, until that partner starts to feel resentful of that sparkle. Once they've used up all you can give them, they try to dim the bright light inside you. But, of course, Kacey is living proof that your light can't be dimmed, no matter how hard someone might try to snuff it out.

We all deserve to be with someone who appreciates our shimmer, instead of trying to dim it. If you don't have that someone, appreciate your own shimmer, because I promise you it's bright! Keep sparkling and make this pretty drink to remind yourself that only someone on your level of greatness can handle you.

---

1 ounce whiskey

1 ounce amaretto liqueur

2 ounces cranberry juice

Red edible glitter

Combine the whiskey, amaretto liqueur, cranberry juice, and red edible glitter in a cocktail shaker with ice. Shake well and strain into a shot glass.

Piece of Me

Britney Spears

HOT PINEAPPLE SHOT

Although most of us can't even begin to relate to Britney's journey, we can certainly relate to being fed up with some facet of our life. This song is for that feeling when you just want to scream "YOU WANT A PIECE OF ME?" in the face of anyone who rubs you the wrong way.

The pineapple juice and grenadine in this drink add a little pop-song sweetness to the punch that is the vodka and hot sauce, representative of that part of us that fights back when we've had enough. Throw this drink back and toast to the fire that's inside all of us.

---

1 ounce vodka

1 ounce pineapple juice

Splash of grenadine

Splash of hot sauce

Maraschino cherry

Pour vodka into a tall shot glass. Then add pineapple juice to the glass. Slowly pour grenadine over a barspoon so that it sinks to the bottom of the glass. Add a splash of hot sauce. Garnish with a maraschino cherry.

Fighter

Christina Aguilera

JALAPEÑO POMEGRANATE MIX

I've been bopping to "Fighter" since I was twelve years old. I remember putting *Stripped* in my CD player for the first time in 2002 and feeling like the most empowered middle schooler there ever was. I may have been just a little bit too young to understand the depth of a lot of what Christina was singing, but her words made such an impression on me at that age, and still do today. *Stripped* is all about owning your sexuality (something I can now appreciate as an adult), being a fighter, shouting so your voice is heard, not letting anyone hold you down, and, ultimately, loving yourself.

This drink packs a punch and isn't too sweet, just like this song. The jalapeño syrup offers a little spice, and the pomegranate juice adds a touch of sour and sweet. The lime sparkling water (in case you haven't noticed by now, this is my favorite cocktail topper) gives this cocktail some fizz because we are too fired up to be still.

½ ounce Jalapeño Syrup (page XIV)

1 ounce vodka

3 ounces pomegranate juice

Lime sparkling water

Combine jalapeño syrup, vodka, and pomegranate juice in a cocktail shaker and shake well. Strain into a wineglass over ice and top with lime sparkling water.

Son of a Gun (I Betcha Think This Song Is About You)

Janet Jackson

DRY MARTINI

This my FAVORITE Janet song. I remember when the music video came out in 2001. The vengeful spirit deep down inside me was awakened. Janet takes Carly Simon's "You're So Vain" and makes it darker and angrier. She says what we all wish we could say to that vain motherf*cker we all know, the one who thinks they can get away with cycling through women like a deck of cards.

This drink is dark, dry, and simple. When you're enraged, you need something iconic (like a dry martini) paired with an iconic song by an iconic queen who makes you feel like a bad bitch.

Black gel food coloring (for decorating the glass)

2½ ounces dry gin

½ ounce vermouth

Cracked ice

Green olive (for garnish)

Decorating the glass:

Decorate the inside of your martini glass with black food gel. Get creative! Draw swirls, drips, whatever your heart tells you. You can also line the rim. Set aside.

Cocktail:

Pour the gin and vermouth into a cocktail shaker over ice and shake well. Strain into the decorated martini glass. The drink will turn black from the food gel. Scoop cracked ice into the drink. Garnish with a green olive.

That Don't Impress Me Much
Shania Twain
PINEAPPLE-RUM FRUIT PUNCH COCKTAIL

Shania calls out self-obsessed men in this song, saying she isn't impressed by any of them. It's the perfect light note to end this chapter with because while it stems from a place of fury, it's transitioning into the healing phase.

This drink is fun, fruity, and the perfect poolside beverage for when you're done being angry and you're chilling by the pool without a care in the world. Nothing impresses you, especially not self-absorbed men.

1½ ounces white rum

4 ounces fruit punch

2 ounces pineapple juice

½ ounce grenadine

Pineapple wedge (for garnish)

Pineapple leaves (for garnish)

Maraschino cherry (for garnish)

Pour white rum, fruit punch, pineapple juice, and grenadine into a mixing glass and stir. Pour the mixture into a highball glass over ice. Garnish with a pineapple wedge, pineapple leaves, and a maraschino cherry.

HEALING

Healing is a never-ending journey. I continue to heal from different phases of life as I age, and when I stop to take stock and it all feels overwhelming, I can always count on these songs to remind me that I still have a light shining inside me. I hope these song-and-cocktail pairings offer you peace as you enter the healing phase of a major life event. Life throws so many lemons at you, so gather them all up and put them in a cocktail.

PLAYLIST

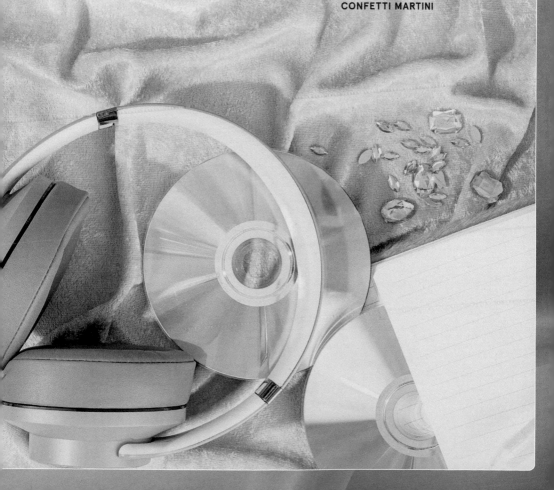

Bejeweled

Taylor Swift

MIDNIGHT BLUEBERRY GIN COCKTAIL (3 A.M. VERSION)

This is the ultimate healing bop! As a mom who works from home and thus rocks a permanent sweatpants wardrobe, frequently covered in snot, this song reminds me that I *can* still make the whole place shimmer. It's so fun, lighthearted, and uplifting—to me, it's the best pump-up song to kick-start a healing night out (or in).

No matter what has been making you feel that you aren't shining, this song is here to remind you that you "polish up real nice." The blue color of this drink encompasses the midnight blue of the *Midnights* album. Pour this simple cocktail and dance the night away, even after the clock strikes midnight. Maybe even until 3 a.m. You never know what surprises await you.

1½ ounces Blueberry Syrup (page XIV)

Midnight blue edible glitter

1½ ounces gin

½ ounce lemon juice

Club soda

Pour blueberry syrup, edible glitter, gin, and lemon juice into a cocktail shaker. Shake well, then strain into a cocktail glass. Top with club soda.

I'm Trying (Not Friends)

Maisie Peters

LEMON DROP SHOT

Let's be honest: Every healing journey encounters bumps in the road from our own conflicting thoughts and beliefs. When someone hurts us, we try to find excuses for their behavior because it's too hard to leave. We wait around for apologies that never come, we go through periods of self-loathing, we argue with the person in our heads, we even plead with them about why we weren't good enough. One minute we're plotting their demise in our dreams, the next we're wishing they'd just love us again.

Then one day, like magic, we simply feel indifferent.

This song is about that push and pull. In the lyrics, Maisie mentions lemon drops, so what *else* would I pair it with? This concoction is easy to make, it's sweet, and it goes down so easy. Take this delicious shot and appreciate being lost because it's okay to be confused. This recipe yields five shots, for your "healthy five" friends.

---

5 ounces freshly squeezed lemon juice, plus more for rimming the glasses

Granulated sugar (for rimming the glasses)

5 ounces vodka

5 sugar cubes

Yellow edible glitter

5 lemon slices (for garnish)

Sugar rims:

Squeeze some lemon juice into a bowl. Sprinkle some sugar onto a plate.

Dip the rim of each shot glass into the lemon juice, then dip it into the sugar to rim the glass.

Shots:

Combine vodka, 5 ounces of lemon juice, sugar cubes, and yellow edible glitter in a cocktail shaker and shake well (until the sugar has dissolved). Strain into shot glasses. Top with lemon slices.

thank u, next
Ariana Grande
PALOMA

I remember that, right before this song came out, everyone expected Ariana to be bitter about her breakup with Pete Davidson, but she flipped the script and came out with this banger, showing gratitude to her exes instead. It's empowering to think of how our exes have helped us grow, even if the relationships were horrible in some ways. Ari also reminds me that it's *me* I should be thanking the most, as I'm the one who has handled all the pain and loss and come out still standing.

Making this drink is even easier than getting over your ex. If you hate the taste of liquor, mask it with grapefruit—that always works! And simple syrup is easy to make or find in stores. This drink is a simple sweet-and-sour combination.

2 ounces grapefruit juice, freshly squeezed

½ ounce lime juice

½ ounce Simple Syrup (page XIII)

1½ ounces tequila

Club soda

Grapefruit peel and/or grapefruit wedge

Combine grapefruit juice, lime juice, simple syrup, and tequila in a cocktail shaker. Shake well, then strain into a coupe glass. Top with club soda. Garnish with a grapefruit peel and/or a grapefruit wedge.

Lose You To Love Me
Selena Gomez
DISTORTED ESPRESSO MARTINI

Letting a toxic person go is the ultimate act of self-love. It can be so painful and sometimes it might even feel that you won't survive, but often you'll come out on the other side stronger than ever. All the love that was once directed toward that person is now aimed back at your own heart. It can take a long time, but the journey is worth it.

Mourning a person we've lost can be exhausting, so what better way to counteract that exhaustion than an espresso martini? Make this drink to give yourself a little burst of energy to close that chapter that is no longer serving you.

---

2 ounces vodka

½ ounce Kahlua

1 ounce espresso (freshly brewed or bottled)

½ ounce Simple Syrup (page XIII)

Coffee bean (for garnish; optional)

Combine vodka, Kahlua, espresso, and simple syrup in a cocktail shaker and shake well. Strain into a martini glass. Garnish with a coffee bean (optional).

Special

Lizzo featuring SZA

ORANGE CHAMPAGNE FLOAT

Listening to Lizzo gives me the ultimate confidence boost. The queen of self-love makes me appreciate who I am more than anybody else. It's hard to listen to happy music when I'm feeling unworthy, but this song is the exception. Who better to remind us that we are special than Lizzo herself?

Prosecco screams "I LOVE ME!" to me. This is a celebratory song, and, with this drink, we are celebrating ourselves, ladies! This drink is easy, decadent, and delicious. It makes me feel like I'm truly treating myself when I sip on it.

---

3 ounces orange juice

1 ounce ginger ale

1 ounce prosecco

1 small scoop ice cream or sherbet—whatever flavor floats your boat! (Suggestions: vanilla ice cream or rainbow sherbet)

Mix orange juice, ginger ale, and prosecco in a highball glass and top with ice cream or sherbet.

NOTE:
The measurements for this drink are merely suggestions. This one is all about YOU, so listen to your heart when making it.

Sorry

Beyoncé

LEMON DROP MARTINI

When I first heard the *Lemonade* album, "Sorry" was my instant favorite. I've always been the type of person to do exactly what this song says to do: Go out and forget about the person who hurt me for a little bit and wait to wallow in all my sadness later. Sometimes, in order to heal, you need to unapologetically take what you need and claim some space for yourself.

This is one of my absolute favorite cocktails. I could sip on these all night long—they're easy to make, light, citrusy, and delicious. Of course, the lemon in this drink reflects the title of this album. Whip up this cocktail, throw your middle fingers up, don't pick up the phone, and have the night of your life. BOY, BYE!

---

1 tablespoon ultrafine sugar, plus more to line the rim

6 ounces freshly squeezed lemon juice

2 ounces vodka

Crushed ice

Sugar rim:

Sprinkle some ultrafine sugar onto a plate. Squirt some lemon juice into a bowl. Dip a martini glass into the lemon juice, then roll the glass into the sugar to line the rim.

Cocktail:

Place 1 tablespoon of sugar, lemon juice, and vodka in a cocktail shaker. Vigorously shake for 40 seconds. Strain into a martini glass.

Finely crush ice in a blender, an ice crusher, or a plastic bag using a hammer (get that rage out!). Scoop a little into the martini to float on top.

2 Be Loved (Am I Ready)

Lizzo

RASPBERRY GIN COCKTAIL

Before we dive into love and relationships, we have to ask ourselves: Are we ready? Have we healed enough to love someone else?

In this song, Lizzo asks herself these questions but also points out that it's okay to fall in love without being 100 percent healed. She says it's something she will struggle with her whole life, and I think we can all relate to that. We're all going to go back and forth between self-love and self-loathing at different points, and that's okay.

This pretty purple drink reminds me of the end of the "2 Be Loved" music video. The diamond ice represents the diamonds that we are, even when we don't think we are.

1½ ounces Empress gin

1 ounce Raspberry Syrup (page XV)

Purple edible glitter

½ ounce lemon juice

Club soda

Diamond-shaped ice:
Freeze water in a diamond ice mold overnight.

Cocktail:
Pour Empress gin, raspberry syrup, purple edible glitter, and lemon juice in a wineglass over diamond-shaped ice and stir. Top with club soda.

Clean (Taylor's Version)
Taylor Swift
MINT CUCUMBER VODKA COCKTAIL

Finally getting over something—whether it's a relationship, a job, or a traumatic event—is wonderfully freeing. The road to recovery can be incredibly long and staggering, but the end game is so refreshing. You can finally breathe again. You can finally see clearly again. You are finally back home to yourself.

The combination of mint and cucumber screams "Clean" to me, and this refreshing cocktail goes exceptionally well with this blissfully chill song. Mix this up and drink to your accomplishments, your strength, and your drive. Leaving something you have outgrown is difficult, but you did it, superstar.

6–7 cucumber rounds

½ ounce Mint Syrup (page XV)

1½ ounces freshly squeezed lime juice

2 ounces vodka

Club soda

Mint sprigs (for garnish)

Muddle 4–5 cucumber rounds in a cocktail shaker. Add mint syrup, lime juice, and vodka. Shake well. Strain over ice. Top with club soda. Garnish with mint sprigs and 2 cucumber rounds (or more, if desired).

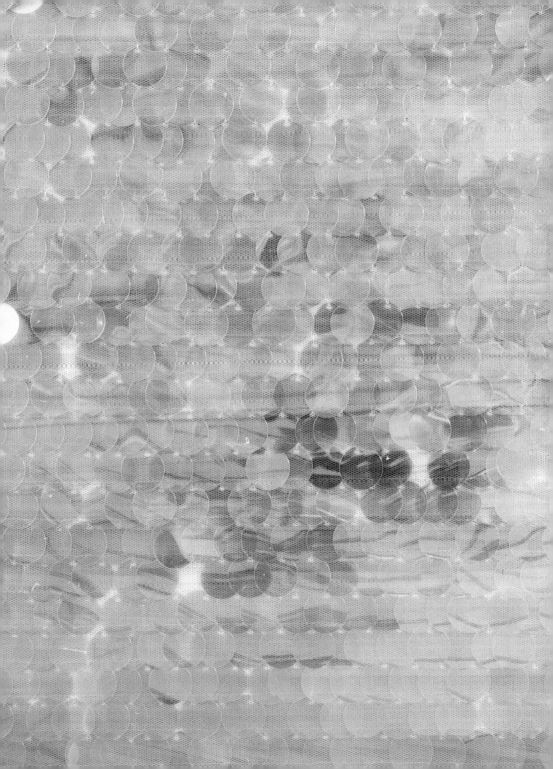

there is a light

Kacey Musgraves

VODKA MARSHMALLOW CONFETTI MARTINI

When the album *star-crossed* came out, I hyper-fixated on this song and played it on repeat for a month straight. It was my healing anthem.

Far too many of us go through traumatic experiences and, in that trauma, some of us hide away from the world, thinking that we don't have the strength to endure any of the hardships that come our way.

We can become reckless, but in that recklessness, we might discover a light glowing inside ourselves. This song gives me confidence in knowing that I have everything I need within myself to survive. That light is power, courage, strength, and tenacity—and it's inside of each and every one of us.

When Kacey played this song on her Star-Crossed tour, confetti shot everywhere, the most beautiful rainbow-colored confetti I've ever seen. I tried to re-create the confetti effect with this drink, the rainbow sprinkles melting beautifully into a multicolored wonder.

Marshmallow creme

Rainbow-colored nonpareil sprinkles

1 ounce vodka

1 ounce vanilla liqueur

1 ounce coconut milk

1 ounce Marshmallow Syrup (page XIV)

NOTE:
I learned this fun, marshmallow creme–nonpareil sprinkle effect from my lovely friend Joanna, @lovelyontheinside on TikTok!

Decorating the glass:

Rim the inside of your martini glass with marshmallow creme. Cover the creme with nonpareil sprinkles.

Cocktails:

Combine vodka, vanilla liqueur, coconut milk, and marshmallow syrup in a cocktail shaker and shake well. Strain into the prepared martini glass. The sprinkles should bleed into the glass, creating a rainbow effect.

CHAPTER

4

CELEBRATION

If you're reading this in order, then you've made it through the grueling chapters of Heartbreak and Fury, and you've done some healing, so now it's time to celebrate, babe! Apply your most sparkly eyeshadow, put on your hottest outfit, and get ready to dance.

These drinks and this chapter are perfect for throwing up your arms, dancing on a table, and cheering yourself on! Turn to this chapter for bachelorette parties, birthday parties, promotions at work, or any other reason you have to celebrate!

PLAYLIST

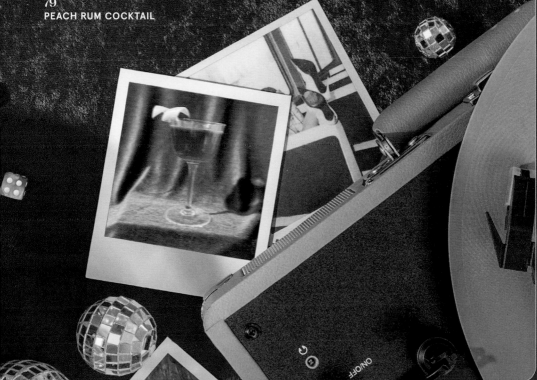

Toxic

Britney Spears

TOXIC RUM SHOT

There must not be a single person on Earth who can resist the urge to dance a little when they hear "Toxic." As soon as that familiar melody hits—you know the one—you *know* Queen Britney is about to take you to another level. "Toxic" is undeniably one of the best pop songs ever made. Its iconic tune and fun lyrics have stood the test of time.

Britney sings about a relationship that might not be good for her but is way too fun to resist. And that's why this "toxic" shot goes perfectly with this legendary song: It's also bright and fun and goes down easy, consequences be damned.

Splash of grenadine

¾ ounce rum

¾ ounce cranberry juice

¾ ounce peach schnapps

¾ ounce freshly squeezed lemon juice

Splash of Sprite

Pour a splash of grenadine into a shot glass and set aside. Mix the rum, cranberry juice, peach schnapps, and lemon juice in a cocktail shaker. Shake well and strain into the shot glass. Top with a splash of Sprite.

ALIEN SUPERSTAR

Beyoncé

GREEN ALIEN MIDORI RUM COCKTAIL

It almost feels wrong to put a song from *RENAISSANCE* on a playlist and take it out of the context of the album because that album is such a cohesive masterpiece, flowing perfectly from start to finish. But I can't resist—when this song comes on, I cannot be stopped. I become another human; my wild side is activated, and nobody can tell me I'm not the hottest bitch in the room. Beyoncé has a masterful way of making women feel empowered, sexy, smart, and UNIQUE, all by unapologetically loving herself.

"ALIEN SUPERSTAR" screams summertime party to me, so I wanted to pair it with something delicious that can be easily sipped by a pool, at a household gathering, or at the club. Whip this up (or make someone whip it up for you, queen!), put on your sexiest summer dress and dance the night away.

---

1 ounce Midori

1 ounce rum

3 ounces pineapple juice

Coconut cream

Pineapple slices

Place the Midori, rum, pineapple juice, and coconut cream in a cocktail shaker. Add ice and shake well. Strain over ice into a collins glass. Garnish with pineapple slices.

Born This Way

Lady Gaga

STAR ANISE–SPICED VODKA COCKTAIL

Lady Gaga has given so many people confidence just by being unabashedly herself. She's never cowered away from her freaky side, and she's always inspired us to embrace ours. Our queen stays unbothered and continuously pushes the envelope effortlessly.

I think this song encompasses what Lady Gaga stands for in the most upfront way. She's simply telling us we are superstars the way we are, and that no matter how badly society wants to shit on us for that, we should celebrate it.

I thank Mother Monster every day for helping so many people tap into their true essence, creativity, and freedom. This drink is sweet with a hint of spice, just like Lady Gaga herself. Make it and celebrate yourself for exactly who you are.

1½ ounces vodka

½ ounce Star Anise Syrup (page XV)

3 ounces freshly squeezed orange juice

Orange slice (for garnish)

Star anise (for garnish)

Maraschino cherry (for garnish)

Combine vodka, star anise syrup, and orange juice in a cocktail shaker. Shake well and strain into a coupe glass. Garnish with an orange slice, star anise, and a maraschino cherry.

girls girls girls

FLETCHER

OLD-FASHIONED

Not only does this song make me want to dance, but it also makes me feel really hot! Pairing the very drink that FLETCHER sings about in the lyrics of this sexy song puts things at level 100.

This classic whiskey cocktail is sometimes stereotyped as a "man's drink," and I love that this song's lyrics reclaim it for the girls, just as FLETCHER reclaims the Katy Perry line "I kissed a girl and I liked it" for the queer community. This drink is pure class, and it's my favorite cocktail to make. Groove to FLETCHER while you prepare this classic cocktail and sip her like an old-fashioned.

---

1 sugar cube

2 dashes bitters

Splash of club soda

2 ounces whiskey

1 orange, peeled and sliced

Maraschino cherries (for garnish)

Place the sugar cube in a rocks glass, then add 2 dashes of bitters. Pour in a tiny splash of club soda. Muddle together until a paste is made. Put a square ice cube in the glass, then top with whiskey. Heat a small slice of orange peel with a match or a lighter and rim the glass with the oil from the orange peel. Throw the peel into the glass. Garnish with maraschino cherries and orange slices.

Juicy
Doja Cat
PEACH RUM COCKTAIL

This song still holds the number-one spot in my Doja Cat ranking. "Juicy" is meant to be blasted as loudly as possible while throwing ass with friends and maybe even strangers. And who doesn't associate peaches with a juicy booty? This peach drink pairs perfectly with Doja's best song. (And if you don't agree with that designation, you can argue with the wall.)

1 ounce peach schnapps

2 ounces white rum

2 ounces freshly squeezed orange juice

1 ounce cranberry juice

Fill a collins glass with ice and add peach schnapps, white rum, and orange juice. Stir well, then top with cranberry juice.

HEATED

Beyoncé

APEROL SPRITZ

Another hot girl summer anthem. This song had me shouting "Uncle Jonny made my dress!" out of nowhere for months. Like all of *RENAISSANCE*, this song makes me feel empowered, hot, and unstoppable. It takes me back to summer pool parties with my best friends, sipping cold drinks in the sun, and laughing the day away.

To pair with it, I chose *the* drink of summer: the Aperol spritz. Because what cools you off better when you're HEATED?! Sip this drink, float in the pool, and relish the fact that you're a powerful goddess.

3 ounces prosecco	Fill a wineglass with a generous amount of ice. Pour Aperol and prosecco into the wineglass. Top with club soda. Garnish with an orange slice.
1 ounce Aperol	
1 ounce club soda	
Orange slice (for garnish)	

positions

Ariana Grande

KIWI VODKA COCKTAIL

I never get tired of "positions." I've heard it literally a trillion times, and it doesn't get old. I don't know what she put in this song to make it so perfect, but if this comes on at a party, I'm performing a chair dance for everyone. (I'm a Leo rising, okay?)

I LOVE a tart drink with a hint of sweetness, and this drink pairs so well with Ariana's little ditty. Make this cocktail and get ready to dance with (or for) your friends.

---

5 slices peeled kiwi

1 teaspoon sugar

½ ounce lime juice

1 ounce vodka

Club soda

Combine kiwi and sugar in a cocktail shaker and muddle them together. Add lime juice and vodka. Shake well, then strain through a mesh strainer. Top with club soda.

I Wanna Dance With Somebody (Who Loves Me)

Whitney Houston

JALAPEÑO GIN COCKTAIL

This is my go-to karaoke song! When I hear it, I see confetti in my mind. It's so poppy, fun, colorful, and upbeat. It's just an ultimate feel-good anthem. The message is simple: Whitney just wants to dance with somebody who loves her. Don't we all? Even people who claim to hate dancing can't help but feel joy when dancing with someone who loves them, right?

I tried to capture the bright colors from this music video and put them into a drink. Make this dazzling cocktail and dance it out with the people you love most.

---

1 ounce Jalapeño Syrup (page XIV)

1½ ounces gin

Gold edible glitter

Splash of grenadine

3 ounces Sprite

Maraschino cherry (for garnish)

Pour jalapeño syrup, gin, and edible glitter in a cocktail shaker. Shake well. Pour a splash of grenadine into the bottom of a coupe glass, then strain the cocktail mixture into the coupe glass. Top with Sprite. Garnish with a maraschino cherry.

Levitating

Dua Lipa

BLOOD ORANGE MARGARITA

I dare you to listen to "Levitating" and try to stop yourself from clapping along with the clapping in the song. It's virtually impossible—when this song comes on, I stop whatever I'm doing for those two claps.

This song is all about dancing under the moonlight, surrounded by glitter and starlight. It makes me feel like I'm on another planet, radiating pink light.

This absolutely delicious drink pairs my favorite fruit—blood orange—with my favorite thing to drink when I want to dance the night away: tequila. Make this drink with your friends before a night on the town or a dance party in your own living room.

About 2 teaspoons salt or sugar (for rimming the glass)

Lime wedge (for rimming the glass)

2 ounces tequila blanco

2 ounces freshly squeezed blood orange juice

1 ounce freshly squeezed lime juice

½ ounce Simple Syrup (page XIII)

Salt or sugar rim:

Pour about 2 teaspoons of salt or sugar onto a plate.

Run a wedge of lime around the top of a rocks glass. Dip the top of the glass into the salt or sugar and roll it from side to side. Fill the glass with ice and set aside.

Cocktail:

Combine tequila blanco, blood orange juice, lime juice, and simple syrup in a cocktail shaker. Shake well. Strain into the prepared rocks glass.

Boys

Charli XCX

BUBBLEGUM COCKTAIL

This song immediately takes me back to my best friend's living room, where she hosted parties when we were in our mid-twenties. I'm dancing with my chosen family, buzzed, happy, and without a care in the world.

Charli herself said she wanted to flip the script with this song, making boys the object of affection rather than girls. In the music video, men are the eye candy rather than women. It's a nice change of pace. Plus, this song is so much FUN.

When I hear "Boys," all I can see is pink. This bubblegum drink pairs perfectly with the bubblegum beat of this song.

---

2 ounces vodka

Pink edible glitter

1½ ounces Bubblegum Syrup (page XIV)

Club soda

Bubblegum (for garnish)

Pour vodka, edible glitter, and bubblegum syrup into a cocktail shaker. Shake well. Strain into a beer can glass over ice and top with club soda. Garnish with bubblegum.

Spice Up Your Life
Spice Girls
STRAWBERRY LOLLIPOP DAIQUIRI

This is my favorite Spice Girls song because it takes me right back to the glitter gel pens, lava lamps, beaded curtains, and inflatable furniture of the late '90s and early 2000s. The song is all about feeling carefree and having fun, just the way we did when we were kids.

When I hear this song, I immediately think of the Spice Girls–branded lollipops they used to sell in the early 2000s. If you're a millennial, like me, you might remember them, too. I always got the strawberry flavor, so naturally I had to make a strawberry cocktail to pair with this iconic song.

This drink is youthful and full of joy. Who doesn't love a strawberry daiquiri? Pairing this with a strawberry lollipop will take you right back to your preteen bedroom.

4 cups frozen strawberries

1 cup fresh strawberries, sliced, plus more for garnish

5 ounces Simple Syrup (page XIII)

4 ounces rum

Juice from 1 lime

Whipped cream (for garnish)

1 strawberry lollipop (for garnish)

Place frozen strawberries, fresh strawberries, simple syrup, rum, and lime juice in a blender and blend until smooth. Pour into a beer can glass and garnish with strawberries, whipped cream, and a strawberry lollipop.

Karma

Taylor Swift

VODKA MIDORI COCKTAIL

Sorry, babe. Karma is my boyfriend. I got mine, but you'll get yours ten times over. This bop of the century illustrates the importance of understanding this *simple* concept. It takes vitriol and turns it into happiness. It's brilliant.

We ALL know a "spider boy" who weaves their "little webs of opacity," aka lies, so pathologically and so poorly that it's laughable. Blast this song and make this delicious and fun cocktail while remembering that while that "spider boy" was meeting up with his ex behind everyone's back, you were self-reflecting and cleaning up your side of the street.

The reason I chose Midori for this drink is simple: Taylor wears bright, sparkly green eyeshadow in the Spotify background for this song, and with the sparkly green of this drink, I wanted to evoke that gorgeously smug aesthetic—not to mention the green monster of envy, the kind of envy someone might feel if karma isn't quite as relaxing a thought for them.

---

1 ounce vodka

1 ounce Midori

1 ounce triple sec

1 pasteurized egg white or ½ ounce aquafaba

1 ounce freshly squeezed lemon juice

Lime sparkling water

Lemon wheel (for garnish)

Maraschino cherries (for garnish)

Combine vodka, Midori, triple sec, egg white or aquafaba, and lemon juice in a cocktail shaker. Dry-shake vigorously for 30 seconds. Add ice, then shake vigorously for another 30 seconds. Strain into a coupe glass. Top with lime sparkling water, then garnish with a lemon wheel and maraschino cherries.

... Baby One More Time

Britney Spears

RASPBERRY GIN COCKTAIL

Is this the most iconic pop song in history? It certainly belongs in that conversation. For me, it isn't even a question: Britney is the queen of pop, and I can't be told otherwise. AND THE MUSIC VIDEO?! The pink feathery hair ties, the schoolgirl outfit, the pencil tapping on the dress—it was an absolute cultural reset and made history.

When I got this album (on cassette) when I was just a little girl myself (nine years old), I couldn't understand the complexity of the loneliness that's killing her, but I memorized every word to the song and every other song on the album anyway. I remember trying to learn the dance from the music video with my besties.

This drink is a light pink color, mimicking the iconic pink hair ties Britney wears in her braided pigtails. It's sweet, just like the illusion of innocence in this song, and it's delicious. Make this drink for your BFFs and scream along with the lyrics because EVERYONE knows every word to this song.

---

5 raspberries

2 ounces gin

1 pasteurized egg white or ½ ounce aquafaba

Juice from ½ lemon

¼ teaspoon vanilla extract

½ ounce agave

Club soda

Muddle 5 raspberries in a cocktail shaker. Add gin, egg white or aquafaba, lemon juice, vanilla extract, and agave. Dry-shake for 30 seconds. Add ice, then shake for another 30 seconds. Strain into a coupe glass. Top with club soda.

CHAPTER
5

COMFORT

I put on this playlist when I'm relaxing with friends on the back deck, in the park, or on a low-key game night, everyone gathered around a table with candles lit. Every song on this list brings me so much peace, and when you play them in order, it's like floating through space on a fluffy, relaxing cloud (especially if you spark up a joint with your cocktail, if that's your thing!). I love making these drinks for my friends, and I hope they'll inspire you to share with your squad, too. Feel free to multiply the recipes accordingly.

PLAYLIST

Good Days

SZA

GRAPEFRUIT AND ELDERFLOWER VODKA COCKTAIL

When I hear this song I think of frost melting, azaleas blooming, butterflies, the sun reflecting through prisms to create rainbows, longer days, and all the hope that spring brings. I can turn this song on in the dead of winter and it's instantly spring in my mind. It's warm, hopeful, and dreamy.

I love to put on this song, make this drink, and escape off into dreamland. For me, that's sitting outside in the sun with my eyes closed. The fresh grapefruit and the elderflower liqueur taste exactly like spring. Make this cocktail and escape to whatever your dreamland is.

2 ounces freshly squeezed grapefruit juice

1 ounce vodka

1 ounce elderflower liqueur

½ ounce freshly squeezed lemon juice

3–4 dashes citrus bitters

Lemon slice (for garnish)

Combine ice, grapefruit juice, vodka, elderflower liqueur, lemon juice, and citrus bitters in a cocktail shaker. Shake well, then strain into a coupe glass. Garnish with a lemon slice.

Sun Bleached Flies

Ethel Cain

VODKA COCONUT COCKTAIL

Yes, *Preacher's Daughter* is an extremely dark album, so it might seem odd that I've decided to include two songs from it in the Comfort chapter. But this song actually comforts me so much that I'm getting a tattoo of its lyrics.

Through the album, the journey taken by the character Ethel embodies comes to a perfect head in this song. It's all about reminding ourselves that even though people hurt us, they have their own battles and trauma that they're also trying to escape from. There's so much hope. Even though Ethel's upbringing and her country have failed her, she still longs for the idealized version of both those things. She also accepts her fate and embraces the peace that comes with death (or, in our case, healing).

The white color of this drink represents the white color of a sun-bleached fly, a gross comparison but delicious nonetheless. Sip this cocktail out in the sun while ascending to the hymnal outro of this heavenly song.

---

1 ounce vodka

½ ounce freshly squeezed lime juice

1 ounce coconut cream

Combine vodka, lime juice, and coconut cream in a cocktail shaker and shake well. Strain in a martini glass.

Rainbow

Kacey Musgraves

RUM RAINBOW FIZZ

"Rainbow" holds such a special place in my heart. When you're feeling anxious, put this song on and feel at peace, at least for a moment, while Kacey reminds us that no matter how hard life gets, there's always a rainbow waiting for us. That, even in the darkness, we can look forward to the light ahead.

The drink I chose to pair with this song is rainbow-colored (of course), and it's also one of my favorite drinks ever. It's delicious, easy to sip on, and it tastes like sunshine after the rain.

Imagine being on a rainbow with the sun beating down on your skin; that's what this cocktail tastes like. The light and fruity flavors are like a tropical, warm vacation. The sweetness of the grenadine and orange juice reflect the sweetness in Kacey's voice.

1 ounce grenadine

1 ounce white rum

6 ounces orange juice (store-bought works best for this drink)

3 ounces club soda

Splash of blue curaçao

Dried orange (for garnish)

Pour grenadine into a wineglass over ice. Combine white rum and orange juice in a small pitcher or measuring cup. Pour the mixture slowly over a barspoon into your wineglass. Mix club soda and blue curaçao in a small pitcher or measuring cup. Pour that mixture slowly over a barspoon into your wineglass. Garnish with a dried orange.

Get Free
Lana Del Rey
BIRDS OF PARADISE VODKA–APEROL ORANGE COCKTAIL

It's a tough contest, but I think this is my favorite Lana song. I return to it often when I'm battling a "war in my mind" and need peace. This song was a turning point for me because of its simple message, encouraging me to move out of a heavy headspace and into a lighter one. Of course, that doesn't happen with just the snap of a finger, but it inspired me to do the inner work that I needed to do to have a healthier outlook. If you are struggling, I hope you can find the help you need. If you need words of encouragement, this "modern manifesto" is the perfect motivation.

The instrumental ending of this song with the birds of paradise squawking softly in the background brings me so much relief. The orange juice and orange slice in this drink are reflective of the beautiful orange color of the feathers on a Raggiana bird of paradise.

1½ cups freshly squeezed orange juice

½ ounce freshly squeezed lemon juice

1½ ounces Aperol

1½ ounces vodka

½ ounce Simple Syrup (page XIII)

1 pasteurized egg white or ½ ounce aquafaba

Orange slice (for garnish)

Combine orange juice, lemon juice, Aperol, vodka, simple syrup, and egg white or aquafaba in a cocktail shaker. Shake vigorously for 30 seconds. Add ice, then shake vigorously for another 30 seconds. Strain into a coupe glass. Garnish with an orange slice.

seven
Taylor Swift
BOURBON SWEET TEA

Ah, childhood. When we take a glimpse back in time to those magical days, we unlock core memories, such as climbing trees with the world underneath us, playing near a creek, and the special childhood friendships we had, even if they were brief. And, of course, we picture ourselves as the hope-filled, innocent, naive little kids we once were.

In this song, Taylor comforts another child (or maybe even her inner child), suggesting that this child come and live with her. She proposes that they can be pirates, venturing into a land of make-believe where everything is magical and good. I, personally, listen to this song when my inner child needs healing. When I'm beating myself up for no good reason, I think back to the little girl who took solace in hiding in the woods behind her house. Sometimes she needs to be comforted and reminded that she is loved.

Taylor mentions "sweet tea in the summer," so this is a drink made with sweet tea and bourbon. It is perfect for sipping in the summer, surrounded by friends and/or family whom you love "to the moon and to Saturn." This recipe makes enough for a pitcher to share now or store in your fridge in a sealed container.

---

5 cups water

2 black tea bags

1 cup sugar

4–5 lemon slices

6 ounces bourbon

Bring water to a boil, and brew tea for 3–5 minutes. Remove tea bags. Pour tea into a pitcher over ice, then add sugar and lemon slices. Add bourbon and stir.

American Teenager
Ethel Cain
CRANBERRY AND WHISKEY NEBRASKA MULE

I can't exactly pinpoint why "American Teenager" is so comforting to me, but I think it's because I relate to it so deeply. Growing up as an American teenager in the South, as the narrator did, was a mixed bag, to say the least. Grappling with everything that made me "different"—sexuality, mental illness, not being religious—left me feeling ostracized. I hid everything about myself that made me sparkle because I was afraid of the repercussions of being my true self. Anyone who has ever experienced that kind of trauma, especially religious trauma, can find comfort in others who have experienced it, too, and Ethel bravely expresses this feeling throughout the concept album *Preacher's Daughter*. This critically acclaimed album has made me and many others feel way less alone.

Religious trauma is a major theme throughout Ethel's music, and it's present in this song as well. Ethel sings about her "head full of whiskey" while subtly questioning the military-industrial complex, Jesus, and her own sense of self. The red cranberry juice in this cocktail represents the bloodshed, pain, and darkness hiding in this song, masked by a pop beat and melody. The whiskey is the murkiness of the American Dream, the romanticized idea of stability and honor that can be an addictive poison.

2 ounces cranberry juice

1½ ounces whiskey

¾ ounce freshly squeezed lemon juice

1 (12-ounce) bottle ginger beer

Fresh cranberries, dusted with sugar (for garnish)

Combine cranberry juice, whiskey, and lemon juice in a beer can glass. Top with ginger beer. Garnish with fresh cranberries.

Weeds

MARINA

CINNAMON CHAMOMILE HOT TODDY

"Weeds" has comforted me for years. There's something calming about knowing your history will always come back to you. When I feel the intrusive thoughts starting to creep back in, I put on "Weeds" as a weird welcome ceremony. Like, *Hi, you're back, so I might as well make the best of it.*

This hot drink feels good on your throat and in your hands. Chamomile, arguably the most comforting taste ever, mixes well with the whiskey and cinnamon. I hope it brings you some comfort just as it does for me.

Spiced Cinnamon Syrup (page XV)

1 bag chamomile tea

1½ ounces whiskey

¼ ounce freshly squeezed orange juice

2–3 cinnamon sticks (for garnish)

1–2 orange slices (for garnish)

Boil water in a small saucepan or teakettle. Pour spiced cinnamon syrup into the bottom of an Irish coffee mug. Pour hot water over the syrup, then place the tea bag into the mug and let it steep for 3–5 minutes. Pour in whiskey and freshly squeezed orange juice. Garnish with cinnamon sticks and orange slices.

Stoned at the Nail Salon

Lorde

VODKA MULE

When I hear this song, I want to lie down on the grass, look up at the clouds, and think about how grateful I am for the life I have. I reflect back on my wild, carefree days—I miss them, but the peace I have now is better than anything I've left behind.

There's something so comforting about songs that give you advice. I love the lyric "Spend all the evenings you can with the people who raised you." It reminds me to make time for the wonderful people who made me who I am.

This cocktail is *easy* to make, so whip up a few for the people you love the most, maybe even the people who raised you. Ginger is such a nostalgic flavor; it reminds me of sick days from school spent at home on the couch with ginger ale and the nurturing presence of my mother. The ginger, mixed with the sweetness of the blue curaçao, perfectly encapsulates the feelings this song ignites.

Juice from ½ a lime

2 ounces vodka

1 ounce blue curaçao

1 (12-ounce) bottle ginger beer

Lime wheel (for garnish)

Combine lime juice, vodka, and blue curaçao in a beer can glass. Top with ginger beer. Garnish with a lime wheel.

cowboy like me
Taylor Swift
PERSIMMON AND BOURBON OLD-FASHIONED

It doesn't matter what I'm going through; "cowboy like me" brings me instant comfort. It's so heartwarming to think about finding someone like you, whoever that may be. Finding commonalities in each other brings us a sense of community, love, acceptance, and home.

This song just sounds like an old-fashioned, but with a hint of persimmon, which is why I decided to zhuzh up the classic drink with a persimmon syrup. Persimmons are comforting for me because of my grandmother's persimmon pudding, but their flavor could bring comfort to anyone. Settle down, turn on your twinkle lights, get some candles going, and sip this sweet, soothing cocktail.

---

1 ounce bourbon

1½ ounces Persimmon Syrup (page XV)

1 ounce freshly squeezed orange juice

½ ounce Cointreau

2–3 dashes spiced orange bitters

Persimmon or orange slice (for garnish)

Pour bourbon, persimmon syrup, orange juice, Cointreau, and spiced orange bitters into a mixing glass and stir. Pour into a coupe glass. Garnish with a persimmon or orange slice.

LONGING

L onging can be an exciting feeling at the start of a new relationship or the painful yearning felt when you aren't getting everything you want and need from one. This playlist tells the story of the beginning stages of longing for someone to the end stages when you know it's not *really* over yet, or maybe it is and you've had to accept it.

Put this playlist on when you're looking through old pictures, replaying old memories, or desperately hoping that there will be a next time.

PLAYLIST

Green Light
Lorde
MIDORI SOUR

I remember hearing "Green Light" for the first time in 2017 and feeling so *alive*. Lorde really outdid herself with the album *Melodrama* and cemented her place among the greatest alt-pop girls of our time. Not only do the lyrics of "Green Light" encompass the feeling of longing, but the tempo does as well, rising as the yearning becomes greater and greater. This song feels like running: You start at a slow, steady pace, but then you pick up speed until you're full-on sprinting toward the person you long for. When this song kicks into high gear, you feel like you're there with Lorde as her resentment and desire for her muse commingle. Sometimes, even though we know we should let go of someone, the passion is just too intense, and we keep going back. It's chaotic, confusing, and vibrant.

Of course, this cocktail had to be green. It would be silly to make it any other color. This sour and sweet conflicting combination goes perfectly with the clashing emotions experienced in this song. Whip one up and give yourself permission to do the thing you know isn't right, but is fun. Go ahead, text your ex just this once. Lorde gives you permission.

2 ounces Midori

1 ounce vodka

½ ounce freshly squeezed lime juice

½ ounce freshly squeezed lemon juice

Green edible glitter

2 ounces club soda

Maraschino cherry (for garnish)

Lime slice (for garnish)

Pour Midori, vodka, lime juice, lemon juice, and edible glitter into a highball glass and stir. Top with club soda. Garnish with a maraschino cherry and a lime slice.

Run Away With Me

Carly Rae Jepsen

GRAPEFRUIT MARGARITA

Carly Rae Jepsen's *Emotion* might be the most underrated album of all time. She is the dream-pop queen—you can't convince me otherwise—and this song is the absolute dreamiest. It takes me back to new romance: heart racing, sweaty palms, feeling excited over even the smallest touch. The world looks better through Carly's swirling rose-colored glasses.

Make this cocktail and daydream about your crush. In my opinion, grapefruit is the best juice to mask liquor, so you won't taste much of the tequila. Still, try not to have one too many while your head is in the clouds.

---

2 ounces tequila

1 ounce orange liqueur

1 ounce freshly squeezed grapefruit juice

¾ ounce freshly squeezed lime juice

Place tequila, orange liqueur, grapefruit juice, and lime juice in a cocktail shaker and shake well. Strain over ice.

Her Body Is Bible
FLETCHER
HOLY WATER HIBISCUS MARGARITA

FLETCHER is a genius—comparing romantic longing to a religious experience is just inspired. The metaphor of her lover being her bible, rather than the actual Bible, is so powerful for so many reasons. We can all relate to having a new experience finally feeling right, as if it's the feeling we've been searching for our whole lives, giving us a purpose and something to worship. Amen to freeing ourselves and celebrating ourselves and our loves just the way they are.

This drink is sweet and tart. It probably won't make you have a religious experience like FLETCHER's muse, but it'll definitely get you tipsy! Make this drink and fantasize about *your* muse.

---

1 ounce freshly squeezed lime juice, plus more for rimming the glass

Salt (for rimming the glass)

2 ounces tequila blanco

1 ounce Hibiscus Syrup (page XIV)

Hibiscus flower (for garnish)

Lime slice (for garnish)

Salt rim:
Line the rim of a rocks glass with lime juice. Pour salt into a bowl and stick the rim of the glass into the salt.

Cocktail:
Combine tequila, 1 ounce of lime juice, and hibiscus syrup in a cocktail shaker and shake well. Strain into the prepared rocks glass. Garnish with a hibiscus flower and a lime slice.

ALL UP IN YOUR MIND

Beyoncé

COCONUT-PINEAPPLE MARGARITA

Have you ever heard that some songs cast magic spells? If that's true, then this song *definitely* casts a spell. Play it when you want to be all up in someone's mind. Even if it doesn't work, repeating these powerful lyrics to yourself like a mantra will make you feel like the hottest there ever was.

This song makes me feel the same way tequila makes me feel, so it's only fitting to pair it with a dressed-up tequila shot.

½ ounce freshly squeezed lime juice, plus more for rimming the glass

Turbinado sugar (for rimming the glass)

2 ounces tequila

1 ounce pineapple juice

¼ ounce Cointreau

2 ounces cream of coconut

Pineapple slice (for garnish)

Sugar rim:
Rim a margarita glass with lime juice and then dip it in turbinado sugar.

Cocktail:
Pour tequila, pineapple juice, lime juice, Cointreau, and cream of coconut into a cocktail shaker. Shake well and strain into the prepared margarita glass. Garnish with a pineapple slice.

Delicate

Taylor Swift

BLUE COCONUT RUM

We've all been there . . . that time in a relationship when everything feels delicate, when you're afraid to say or do too much too soon for fear of ruining everything. It's an especially vulnerable stage; if you put all your cards on the table, you could turn them away. If you do nothing, you look uninterested. The song "Delicate" is perfect for the dreamlike haze of the beginning of a relationship when promises aren't being made yet, "but you can make me a drink."

I wanted this cocktail to be similar to the iconic teal blue dress Taylor wears in the "Delicate" music video.

¾ ounce lime juice

¾ ounce blue curaçao

1½ ounces coconut milk

1½ ounces white rum

Orange slice (for garnish)

Place lime juice, blue curaçao, coconut milk, and white rum in a cocktail shaker. Shake well and strain into a highball glass. Garnish with an orange slice.

Bad Romance

Lady Gaga

JALAPEÑO-LIME VODKA COCKTAIL

It's difficult to pinpoint exactly which song is Gaga's most iconic, but, for me, it's "Bad Romance." When this song came out, EVERYONE was talking about it. It felt like there wasn't a single person who hadn't at least seen snippets of the music video, and, by this point, everyone knew who Gaga was and what she stood for. This was the song that pulled me into her web.

Gaga sings about a toxic but irresistible relationship, something far too many of us can relate to. Maybe we were naive and didn't know it was bad for us, but we confused that exciting rush for love and it became an addiction. Gaga paints that picture of a woman addicted to the pain that someone else causes her because the crumbs of affection in the relationship make her long for more.

This drink isn't as hot as pining for that toxic fool, but it has the perfect amount of spicy. It's crisp and simple, and it's perfect to sip on for any occasion.

Splash of grenadine

½ ounce Jalapeño Syrup (page XIV)

2 ounces vodka

Juice of 1 lime

Lime sparkling water

Jalapeños (for garnish)

Red rose (for garnish)

Pour a splash of grenadine into the bottom of a chilled martini glass. Pour jalapeño syrup, vodka, and lime juice into a cocktail shaker. Shake well, then strain into the chilled martini glass. Top with lime sparkling water. Garnish with jalapeños and a red rose.

Hands To Myself

Selena Gomez

JALAPEÑO-WATERMELON MARGARITA

Selena Gomez has so many underrated bops, this being one of them. I can listen to this song on repeat without getting tired of it. It never gets old! It's full of sass and sexy teasing. Selena sings as if she can't keep her hands to herself, but then playfully drops, "I mean I could but why would I want to?" in the bridge. This song reminds me of how much power we can hold in the beginning of a relationship. Selena is calling the shots in this song, and that's how I prefer to operate as well.

This is one of the most refreshing drinks I've ever made. The sweet fresh watermelon and spicy jalapeño syrup marry each other perfectly, just as the downs and the uppers make love to each other in the song. Go get a whole watermelon from the store and make a few of these because I doubt you'll be able to stop yourself after having just one. I mean, you could, but why would you want to?

5-6 watermelon cubes

1½ ounces tequila blanco

1½ ounces lime juice

1½ ounces Jalapeño Syrup (page XIV)

¼ ounce Cointreau

Watermelon slice (for garnish)

Muddle watermelon cubes in a cocktail shaker. Pour in tequila blanco, lime juice, jalapeño syrup, and Cointreau. Shake well. Strain into a rocks glass. Garnish with a watermelon slice.

Curious
Hayley Kiyoko
MANGO-PINEAPPLE RUM COCKTAIL

This song is all about pining for someone who's already in a relationship/situationship/whatever-you-want-to-call-it with someone else. The pining that comes with that forbidden longing. Hayley turns the confusion into a cute question, stating that she's just curious, downplaying the deep emotions hidden behind needing to know, "Is it serious?" We ALL know what it's like to try to play it cool when we long for someone. Hayley even goes on to sing about how she can handle it if the person she longs for is in a serious relationship, almost as if she were trying to convince *herself*. We've all tried to convince ourselves that we don't care when we really do.

I wanted a fun drink for this one. The rum, mango, and pineapple were made for each other. You don't have to be curious about this drink being serious—don't worry, it isn't. It's super easy to make and you don't have to be precise with measurements. So when you're on your second or third one, just pour what your heart tells you to. Who has time to measure when you're having so much fun?

---

2 ounces rum

2 ounces mango juice

2 ounces pineapple juice

Splash of grenadine

Combine rum, mango juice, and pineapple juice in a cocktail shaker. Shake well, then strain into a rocks glass. Slowly pour a splash of grenadine over a barspoon so that it sinks to the bottom.

Like a Prayer

Madonna

VERY DIRTY MARTINI WITH BLUE CHEESE OLIVES

"Like a Prayer" is all about how heavenly it is to long for someone. Madonna spends the full 5 minutes and 42 seconds blissfully pining for her special someone and crooning about that feeling when just hearing the person say your name can make the hairs on your neck stand straight up. It feels like you're up in the heavens and nothing can bring you back down to Earth. It's such a rush.

A well-made dirty martini is the most heavenly cocktail to me, and the drink is almost as iconic as Madonna herself. (Not to mention that the lyrics of this song can be a bit dirty, too, depending on how you interpret them.) Add blue cheese–stuffed olives and you have fully ascended to the heavens above.

---

2 ounces olive juice (from an olive jar)

1½ ounces vodka

Cracked ice (for topping)

Blue cheese–stuffed olives (for garnish)

Chill a martini glass in the freezer (optional).

Honestly, when I make a dirty martini, I let my heart tell me how much olive juice and vodka to put in. Combine olive juice and vodka in a cocktail shaker with ice and shake well. Strain into the chilled martini glass. Pour cracked ice over the top. Garnish with blue cheese olives.

Silk Chiffon

MUNA, Phoebe Bridgers

CHERRY VODKA FIZZ

I love to play this song on a warm, sunny day while sipping a light cocktail and daydreaming. The sapphic energy in this song makes me feel like I'm flying; it's pure queer joy, and that sound is so validating.

The cherry flavor of this drink goes perfectly with the "cherry lipstick" the muse wears in this song, and the vodka gives a little buzz, reminiscent of that very first crush.

---

1 ounce cherry syrup from maraschino cherry jar

1 ounce vodka

½ ounce freshly squeezed lemon juice

Club soda

Maraschino cherries (for garnish)

Combine cherry syrup, vodka, and lemon juice in a beer can glass. Top with club soda. Garnish with maraschino cherries.

august

Taylor Swift

LAVENDER LEMONADE

Is there a song that embodies longing more than "august"? This song is for anyone who has made someone or something their everything, only to find out that person considered them merely an option. I put on "august" when I want to reminisce about times when my hope for what could be kept me going. This is also a song of acceptance—when you're looking back on a romance with fondness mingled with the knowledge that it was never really yours.

This drink tastes like summer love. The lemon is cooling and refreshing, with a touch of romantic lavender, a flower I think Augustine would appreciate.

Dried edible flowers

1½ ounces gin

3 ounces lemonade

½ ounce Lavender Syrup (page XIV)

About 1 ounce butterfly pea tea (see Note)

Flower ice:
Place dried edible flowers into an ice cube tray with water and freeze overnight.

Cocktail:
In a cocktail shaker, combine gin, lemonade, and lavender syrup. Shake for 20 seconds. Strain over flower ice into a beer can glass (or your glass of choice). Slowly pour butterfly pea tea on top of the cocktail to add color.

NOTE:
When brewing butterfly pea tea, only let it brew for about 1 minute. Otherwise, the flavor of the tea will be too strong and will overpower the flavor of the cocktail.

Teenage Dream
Katy Perry
VANILLA-MINT VODKA CANDY DREAM

This is the cutest, sweetest, song about longing I've ever heard. Some argue that "Teenage Dream" is one of the books of the Pop Bible and I have to agree, because this song still has the same effect it had on me when it came out in 2010. The visuals in this album are supreme. When I listen to this song, I'm immediately transported to a cotton candy beach with peppermint-flavored water and lollipops poking out of the sand. I can feel the sun on my skin while I sip cocktails all day long with my lover, basking in the daze of yearning. Then we retire to the motel room to make forts (out of sheets, of course).

This drink is full of candy and whipped cream; I tried to emulate the emblematic candy world Katy created with this album. It's full of sugar, mirroring the sweet beginning of a new relationship.

Marshmallow creme

Pop Rocks (for rimming the glass, optional; may be replaced with sanding sugar)

1½ ounces vodka

1 ounce Vanilla Syrup (page XV)

1½ ounces peppermint schnapps

3 ounces coconut milk (you could also use oat milk)

Whipped cream (for garnish)

Peppermint candy or candy canes (for garnish)

Sprinkles (for garnish)

Cotton candy (for garnish)

Lollipops (for garnish)

Pop Rocks/sugar rim:
Line the rim of a martini glass with marshmallow creme. Pour Pop Rocks or sanding sugar onto a plate and roll the rim of the glass in the sugar until it's fully covered. Set aside.

Cocktail:
Combine vodka, vanilla syrup, peppermint schnapps, and coconut milk in a cocktail shaker and shake well. Strain into the prepared martini glass. Garnish with whipped cream, peppermint candy, candy canes, sprinkles, cotton candy, lollipops, or whatever candy your heart desires.

Lavender Haze
Taylor Swift
HAZY LAVENDER GIN SOUR

While this bop might be anti-marriage, it's pro-love and longing. I think the meaning of this song is completely up to interpretation by the listener and it can be taken many ways. But, to me, it's all about shutting others out while you stay in your love haze with that special person.

Lavender is a historically queer color (see: the Lavender Scare, the Lavender Menace, lavender marriages), so one listener response to this song is about the way it can evoke queer longing, staying in that bubble of two before everyone else finds out and starts to throw stones.

Of course, I chose a lavender drink made with lavender syrup for this cocktail. I wanted this drink to be lavender-flavored, sweet, and a little murky (thanks to the egg white), just like the haze of a new relationship.

---

2 ounces Empress gin

¼ ounce Lavender Syrup (page XIV)

½ ounce freshly squeezed lemon juice

½ ounce Simple Syrup (page XIII)

1 pasteurized egg white or ½ ounce aquafaba

Food-grade lavender

Combine gin, lavender syrup, lemon juice, simple syrup, and egg white or aquafaba in a cocktail shaker. Dry-shake vigorously for 30 seconds. Add ice and shake for another 30 seconds. Strain into a coupe glass and garnish with food-grade lavender.

LOVE

The best love wraps you up like a blanket fresh from the dryer with its soothing weight and warmth. It brings you soup when you're sick. It's the definition of home. You can always feel it—it's all-encompassing, gentle, and easy.

The songs in this chapter evoke the healthiest kind of love, the kind that feels light, soft, cozy, and protective. Many of the songs in the other chapters of this book ultimately lead here: to love.

After the celebrations and the battles, the longing and the seeking, everyone deserves a safe place to land. Whether it's romantic, platonic, familial, or self-directed, I sincerely hope you have love to go home to.

Put this playlist on when you want to feel the love. The song and drink pairings here are perfect for Valentine's Day, Galentine's Day, wedding anniversaries, friendship anniversaries, date nights, or when you just need to be reminded that true love exists.

PLAYLIST

You Are In Love (Taylor's Version)

Taylor Swift

SNOW-GLOBE RUM COCKTAIL

This is my absolute favorite love song of all time. The production is so cinematic and the lyrics are wonderfully vivid. It just sounds like what love feels like. In this album track from *1989*, Taylor highlights how you can feel love in the simplest of moments.

This song takes me back to that first feeling of longing for someone you newly love: the slightest touch, like shoulders brushing, is so exciting. When things are still new, when neither of you can admit how you feel yet, but you're so comfortable together and you know they're feeling it, too. Taylor really put love into the perfect words and somehow the perfect sound as well.

When I hear this song, I picture two people dancing in snow with a blue light behind them. I tried to capture that blue in the color of this drink, and added the white to represent the snow. This drink is sweet and easy, just the way love should be.

Butterfly pea tea

1½ ounces rum

1 ounce blue curaçao

½ ounce white crème de cacao

½ ounce half-and-half

Rose-shaped ice:
Brew butterfly pea tea. Pour the tea into a rose ice mold and freeze overnight.

Cocktail:
Pour rum, blue curaçao, crème de cacao, and half-and-half into a cocktail shaker. Shake well and strain into a coupe glass over the rose-shaped ice.

I Will Always Love You
Dolly Parton/Whitney Houston
RASPBERRY ROSE GIN FIZZ

Sometimes the best thing we can do for someone we love is to give them space. This song captures that heart-wrenching feeling: stepping away from someone and still having unconditional love for them from afar. We love them through our memories of them and for the ever-present feeling of love that will always be there. Dolly wrote the original about leaving the *Porter Wagoner Show*; she knew she had to leave, but she also knew she'd always love the man who believed in her and helped her start her career. Whitney Houston's version is just as powerful, sending chills down my spine every single time I listen to her perfectly belt it out. This song ages like the finest wine. It's a song that's saying "No hard feelings" in the most powerful way possible.

It might be cliché, but roses are the most romantic flower. They symbolize love in so many forms, and their many different colors reflect all the different kinds of love. A pink rose, to me, is the ultimate symbol of love, so I included rose syrup and rose petal garnishes in this drink. Make this cocktail and bask in the love you have in your life.

4–5 fresh raspberries

¼ ounce Rose Syrup (page XV)

1½ ounces gin

Club soda

Food-grade rose petals (for garnish)

Muddle raspberries in the bottom of a stemless wineglass and set aside.

Pour rose syrup and gin in a mixing glass and stir until combined. Add ice to the wineglass with the muddled raspberries. Pour the rose syrup and gin mixture into the wineglass over the muddled raspberries and ice. Top with club soda. Garnish with food-grade rose petals.

Golden Hour

Kacey Musgraves

GOLDEN WHISKEY-LEMON COCKTAIL

"Golden Hour" is another song from Kacey's incredible album of the same name that is dear to my heart because we used to sway our daughter to sleep to it. The most beautiful thing about Kacey's lyrics is that they can apply to anyone, and, in my case, my daughter is my golden hour. Kacey's soft voice transports me back to those early days when my daughter was a baby, and I was holding her close, and she reminded me that everything was gonna be alright.

My daughter is the greatest love I'll ever know, and she has changed me into a more golden version of myself. This drink is simple and sweet, just like that pure and unconditional love. The whiskey is masked by the citrus and the hint of agave.

---

2 ounces whiskey

1 tablespoon freshly squeezed lemon juice

3 ounces freshly squeezed orange juice

1 teaspoon agave

Gold edible glitter

Pour whiskey, lemon juice, orange juice, agave, and edible glitter into a cocktail shaker. Shake well and strain into a coupe glass.

Love song

Lana Del Rey

GOLD WHISKEY HONEY

This is undeniably one of Lana's sweetest songs. Tender violin sounds open the song, and then Lana begins to croon to us. I get chills every single time I listen to it. Love should make you feel like a star, like you are once in a lifetime, because you are. You deserve to be seen for your truest self. You deserve safety. These are the pillars of a healthy love.

This song sounds like gold, so the whiskey, honey, and gold flakes represent the golden love we all deserve.

1½ ounces whiskey

¾ ounce honey

1 ounce Peach Syrup (page XV)

¾ ounce freshly squeezed lemon juice

1 pasteurized egg white or ½ ounce aquafaba

Peach slice (for garnish)

Edible gold flakes (for garnish)

Combine whiskey, honey, peach syrup, lemon juice, and egg white or aquafaba in a cocktail shaker. Dry-shake vigorously for 30 seconds. Add ice and shake vigorously for another 30 seconds. Strain into a coupe glass. Garnish with a peach slice and edible gold flakes.

Sweet Nothing

Taylor Swift

GRAPEFRUIT GIN FIZZ

This is such a romantic song, but its messages can apply to all forms of love. When I heard it for the first time, I sobbed because of how strongly it reminded me of the people in my life who love me so much and ask for nothing in return; the sweet few who I can admit everything to, and they still love me regardless. I think of my mom, my husband, my dog, and my best friends, and I wonder what I did to get so lucky. Being able to relate to this song in any sense is a blessing.

This drink is a coupe glass of sweet nothings. The simple syrup perfectly balances out the tartness of the grapefruit to create a sweet, gulpable drink.

---

2 ounces Malfy Gin Rosa

3 ounces freshly squeezed grapefruit juice

1 ounce Simple Syrup (page XIII)

1 pasteurized egg white or ½ ounce aquafaba

Club soda

Edible flowers (for garnish; optional)

Combine gin, grapefruit juice, simple syrup, and egg white or aquafaba in a cocktail shaker. Dry-shake for 30 seconds. Add ice and shake an additional 30 seconds. Strain into a coupe glass. Top with club soda. Garnish with edible flowers, if desired.

Chinese
Lily Allen
SPIKED HOT CHOCOLATE

This song reminds me how you can curl up and rest securely when you're protected by love. Whether we are loving someone from a distance (as Lily does in this song) or we are with them every day, doing the simplest things with them can be what feels the most magical. Ordering Chinese food, making tea, chatting, sleeping, and watching TV can be more than enough. Nothing compares to that feeling of love and safety. Sure, going out for a big date night is lovely, but getting to feel comfortable and be your most authentic self with someone else is the ultimate showcase of love.

Chocolate milk, hot chocolate, and basically chocolate in general are so comforting and feel like the warmth of love. I wanted to pair this song with a drink that is super easy to make, and with something decadent and comforting, because love should feel like all these things.

---

2 ounces Kahlua

½ ounce dark crème de cacao

½ ounce rum

1½ ounces hot chocolate (see Note)

Whipped cream (for topping)

Marshmallows (for garnish)

Chocolate sprinkles (for garnish)

Combine Kahlua, crème de cacao, and rum in a mug and stir. Pour hot chocolate over the rum mixture and stir again. Top with whipped cream, marshmallows, and chocolate sprinkles.

NOTE:
For hot chocolate, you can use store-bought or make your own. If you're using a packet of store-bought hot chocolate, prepare the hot chocolate before pouring over the rum mixture.

Butterflies

Kacey Musgraves

BUTTERFLY GIN AND TONIC

I believe "Butterflies" paints the perfect picture of how love should feel. I play it when I want to feel the warmth of knowing that real love lifts us up, instead of holding us back. We're all familiar with the butterflies you feel in your stomach when you love someone, but this song also reminds us of how love makes us feel when it goes beyond the butterflies: lifted up, powerful, safe, and, of course, loved.

This drink is light and refreshing. It's filled with butterflies, but it's also a solid, tried-and-true recipe (essentially a dressed-up gin and tonic) that you can count on.

About 8 ounces of butterfly pea tea (for ice cubes)

8 ounces tonic water

½ ounce Empress gin

1 ounce lemon juice (or more, depending on your taste)

Butterfly-shaped ice:
Brew butterfly pea tea, let it cool, then pour into a butterfly ice mold. Freeze overnight.

Cocktail:
Place butterfly-shaped ice in a wineglass and pour in tonic water. Top with Empress gin. Pour in lemon juice.

Apple Pie
Lizzy McAlpine
APPLE PIE WHISKEY CIDER

This song sweetly encapsulates that safe feeling you get when you've found your person. That person is home, no matter where you are. Even a cheap, cramped, basement apartment with hand-me-down furniture can be your safest haven if it's shared with your most trusted companion.

I love how Lizzy compares this feeling to apple pie—the ultimate comfort food. I tried turning that apple pie feeling into this cocktail, so drink this with your beloved or a few of your closest friends on your thrifted couch or the dream couch you've saved up for after many years together. This recipe makes 4–5 servings.

1 liter apple cider

1 cup whiskey

3 orange slices

3 cinnamon sticks

2 whole star anise

½ tablespoon allspice

½ teaspoon ground cloves

Whipped cream

Ground cinnamon

Pour apple cider, whiskey, orange slices, cinnamon sticks, star anise, allspice, and cloves into a heavy saucepan. Bring to a boil and simmer on the stove for 2–3 hours. Ladle into a mug and top with whipped cream and ground cinnamon.

✿ **Sip Me, Baby, One More Time**

Leaning On You

HAIM

SOUR APPLE CRANBERRY WHISKEY

Love is being able to depend on someone. I am so lucky to have people in my life I can lean on, even for the simple things: making sure everything is packed for a trip because I'm forgetful, bringing my favorite snacks home for no reason, checking that my car is in good condition because I know nothing about cars, making sure the dogs are fed . . . I could go on and on. This song reminds me of the dependable people I'm so grateful for, and when it comes on, I can't help but feel happiness.

Although whiskey is not my favorite liquor by any means, there is something inherently soothing about it. This drink is soothing and easy to lean on whenever you need a quick pick-me-up.

---

2 ounces whiskey

1 ounce sour apple schnapps

3 ounces cranberry juice

Apple slice (for garnish; optional)

Combine whiskey, sour apple schnapps, and cranberry juice in a wineglass and stir. Garnish with an apple slice (optional).

Adore You

Miley Cyrus

ROMANTIC ROSE GINGER VODKA

The album *Bangerz* is notorious for kicking off Miley's wild girl era, but out of that era came one of the most beautiful love songs of all time. The lyrics are simple, but Miley's powerful and passionate voice belting these words out makes it such a potent ballad. In this song, she sings about her lover making her feel like she's "standing with an army," and that is what love has always felt like to me. When someone truly loves you, they have your back, no matter what, and there is so much internal assuredness that comes with that. You feel like you can take on the world because you have a strong and loving support system.

Roses are notorious for being the most romantic flower, so I decided to go with a rose-flavored drink with a little hint of ginger for spice, because while this song is sweet and romantic, like a rose, Miley always packs a little punch.

---

1 ounce vodka

1 ounce Rose Syrup (page XV)

1 ounce freshly squeezed lemon juice

1 ounce fresh ginger juice

Pink edible glitter

Club soda

Butterfly pea tea

Edible roses (for garnish)

Combine vodka, rose syrup, lemon juice, ginger juice, and pink edible glitter in a cocktail shaker Shake well and strain into a coupe glass. Top with club soda. Pour butterfly pea tea slowly on top to create a purple top. Garnish with edible roses.

Bloody Mary

Lady Gaga

BLOODY MARY

"Bloody Mary" was one of the empowering songs I had on my "Badass Women" playlist back in 2011. Gaga has revealed that this song is about Mary Magdalene, and the folklore is that she was a woman who loved Jesus so much (whether romantically or platonically) that she stood with him during his crucifixion. She was the first to be there when Jesus rose from the dead. Basically, she was a divine superstar, the "ultimate rockstar's girl-friend," as Gaga described her, whose humanity is revealed in this song. But even though the story is remarkable, Mary's conflicting emotions are relatable. Haven't we all had to pretend to be strong during another's hardship for their sake?

What else would I possibly pair with this song besides a Bloody Mary? There are two options for sourcing tomato juice for your Bloody Mary: You can muddle fresh tomatoes and strain out the juice, or you can buy bottled tomato juice from the store. Either way makes a delicious Bloody Mary, in my opinion.

---

4 ounces tomato juice

2 ounces vodka

4 dashes hot sauce

2 dashes Worcestershire sauce

Pinch of salt

Crack of pepper

5 dashes El Guapo Crawfish Boil bitters (optional)

Pinch of celery salt

½ ounce pickle juice

¼ teaspoon horseradish

Garnish with whatever you'd like!
Some ideas: shrimp, pickle, celery, okra

Place tomato juice, vodka, hot sauce, Worcestershire sauce, salt, pepper, bitters, celery salt, pickle juice, and horseradish in a cocktail shaker. Shake well. Strain into a collins glass. Garnish.

Rocket
Beyoncé
STRAWBERRY MARGARITA

We all remember where we were when Beyoncé dropped her first visual album and became the queen of albums. The world actually stopped turning.

It's time to turn up the heat with Beyoncé and her sexiest song (in my opinion). I saved this one for last because it's bound to lead to something a little freaky deaky. Strawberries are known as an aphrodisiac, so enjoy this fresh strawberry cocktail while savoring a lovely evening with Beyoncé and that special someone. This recipe serves two.

3 cups fresh strawberries (tops cut off)

4 ounces tequila

¼ ounce Cointreau

1½ ounces freshly squeezed lime juice

1½ ounces Simple Syrup (page XIII)

Combine strawberries, tequila, Cointreau, lime juice, and simple syrup in a blender. Add ice if you want it frozen and blend well. Pour into 2 margarita glasses.

About the Author

Ashley Gibson is a self-proclaimed amateur craft cocktail artist, pop music connoisseur, and professional Swiftie. She works the nine-to-five corporate life, but her real passion lies in creating beautiful videos detailing the process of making cocktails. She was born and raised in North Carolina, where she adopted her parents' love for '90s pop country. As soon as she could talk, she began performing Dolly and Shania in her family's living room and begged her mother for a Dolly Parton wig. In adulthood, Ashley has been able to marry her love of pop music with her love for craft cocktail making.

 @ashpoursdrinks

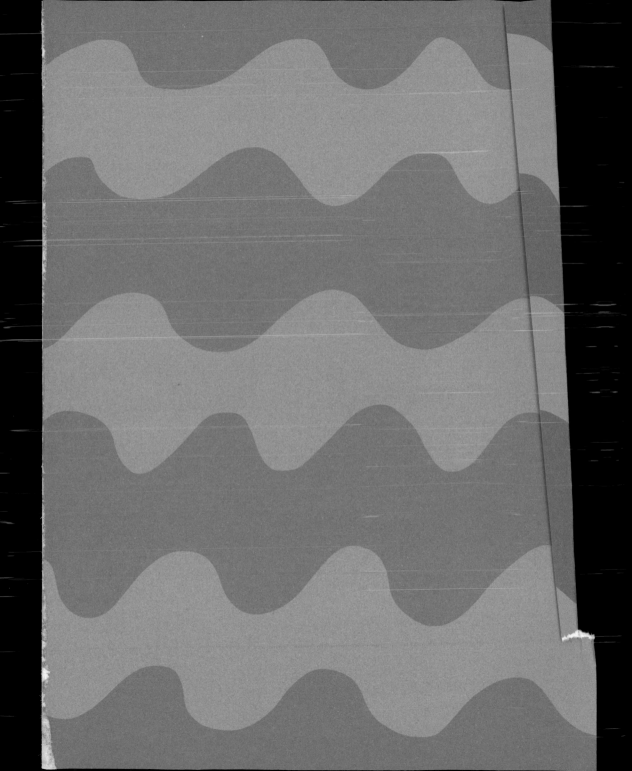

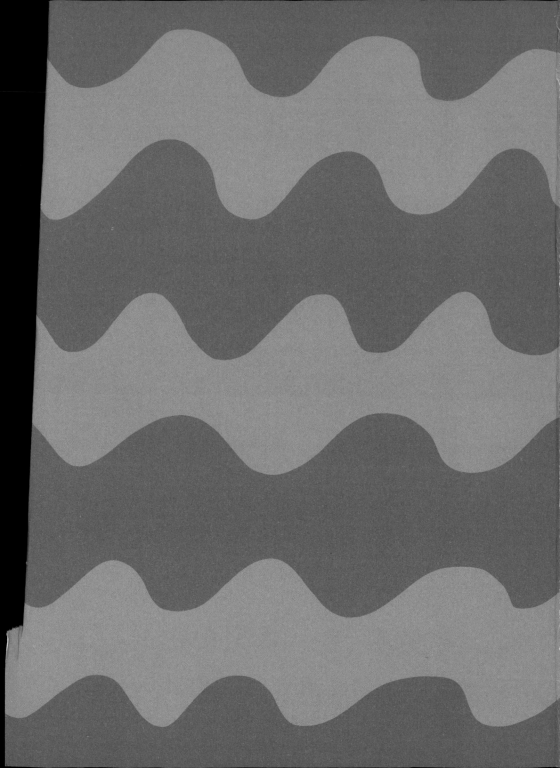